PAUL'S TWO-AGE CONSTRUCTION AND APOLOGETICS

William D. Dennison

Wipf and Stock Publishers
150 West Broadway • Eugene OR 97401
2000

Paul's Two-Age Construction and Apologetics

By Dennison, William A.
Copyright©1985 by Dennison, William A.
ISBN: 1-57910-435-5

Reprinted by *Wipf and Stock Publishers*
150 West Broadway • Eugene OR 97401

Previously published by University Press of America, 1985.

To

Dr. Cornelius Van Til

whose proclamation and faithfulness
to the Truth has been
an inspiration to all his students

ACKNOWLEDGEMENTS

This work was originally written in 1980 as a thesis which met the partial requirements of a Masters of Theology degree at Westminster Theological Seminary in Philadelphia, Pennsylvania. The original title of the thesis was <u>Paul's Two-Age Construction: Its Significance for Apologetics</u>. I have rewritten that thesis into its present form for publication although the content has remained unaltered.

I wish to thank Dr. Harvie Conn, who was the faculty advisor for my thesis at Westminster Theological Seminary. He gave much of his time reading the drafts and made many helpful suggestions. I must also express thanks to my gracious wife, Patricia, who typed the drafts and the final copy of the thesis as the labor of the thesis was carried out.

As I engaged in the project of rewriting the original thesis, I received many insights and helpful suggestions from two very dear friends, Mr. Raymond Haan, my colleague at Calvin Christian High School, and Mrs. Sarah Miller. Each of them spent many hours away from families in order to help one in need. I wish also to express my appreciation to Dr. George Harris of the Classical Languages Department of Calvin College, who kindly transliterated all the Greek words in the text. A special thanks must be given to Mrs. Nancy Milkamp who spent many tedious hours of typing the manuscript in its final form for University Press of America. Thanks must also be directed to Mrs. Rebekah Johnson and Mr. Richard Miller, who typed the revised manuscript for presentation to Mrs. Milkamp. I am responsible for any errors that still remain in the manuscript.

Finally, I am grateful for the strong encouragement I received to carry out this project from Dr. Harvie Conn, Dr. Richard B. Gaffin, Jr., Rev. Charles G. Dennison (my brother), Rev. Gerald S. Taylor, and my wife, Patricia.

Table of Contents

Acknowledgements.. v

Abbreviations... ix

Preface... xi

Chapter 1: Background For Discussing Paul's Two-Age Construction: Plato and Jewish Apocalyptic Literature................................... 1

Chapter 2: Paul's Two Age Construction...................... 27

Chapter 3: I Corinthians 1-3: Antithetical Wisdom..,...... 55

Chapter 4: The Apologetic Significance of the Two-Ages.... 87

Selected Bibliography... 117

Indexes... 119

Abbreviations

DAC   James Hastings, ed. *Dictionary of the Apostolic Church*.
      New York: Charles Scribner's Sons, 1918.

DB   James Hastings, ed. *A Dictionary of the Bible*.
      Edinburgh: T. & T. Clark, 1905.

DBT   Xavier Leon-Dufour, ed. *Dictionary of Biblical Theology*.
      New York: Seabury Press, 1973.

TDNT Gerhard Kittel, ed. *Theological Dictionary of the New Testament*. G. W. Bromiley, trans. and ed. Grand Rapids: Wm. B. Eerdmans, 1964-1976.

ZPEB Merrill C. Tenney, ed. *The Zondervan Pictorial Encyclopedia of the Bible*. Grand Rapids: Zondervan, 1975.

Preface

It is imperative, in my estimation, that the Reformed community reflect fruitfully upon the Vos-Ridderbos-Gaffin interpretation of St. Paul, for a restatement of Reformed theological formulations. Believing theirs to be the correct interpretation of Paul's thought, I deal in this work with the theological discipline of apologetics in terms of Paul's eschatological two-age construction. My purpose is to demonstrate that St. Paul uses the two-age construction as the starting point of a Christian apologetic. To demonstrate this position, I begin by addressing the issue of synthesis. Historically, there are two main perspectives from which synthesis must be seen: 1) the perspective that Christendom has synthesized itself with secular thought and 2) the perspective that the human authors of Scripture were engaged in synthetic thought. Christianity's relationship with Plato will serve as an example of the former,[1] whereas Paul's assumed relationship with Jewish apocalyptic literature will serve as an example of the latter. These are the only two representative conceptions of synthesis I address, though I am aware of the very broad, yet complicated and scholarly discussion of snythesis. Such a thorough discussion is too lengthy to concern us here, however. The two examinations mentioned previously are sufficient to demonstrate, on the basis of Paul's two-age construction, that Christianity is antithetical to any synthesis with secular thought. The points discussed and conclusions reached in this section are basically applicable to the entire discussion on synthesis.

In the second chapter, I immediately direct our attention to Paul's Christocentric eschatology, which is the context for treating the structure of

[1] We can discuss the synthesis respecting Plato in two directions: 1) that the New Testament is influenced by Gnostic elements of which Platonic dualism is a basic ingredient (Bultmann) and 2) that the Church throughout the ages has taken the liberty to have a high respect for Plato and has aligned him with Christian thought. In this work I am much more concerned with the latter, though I will make brief reference to the former. For an excellent criticism of the first position, cf. George Eldon Ladd, The Pattern of New Testament Truth (Grand Rapids: Wm. B. Eerdmans Publishing Company, 1968), pp. 12-40.

his two-age construction. The purpose of the second chapter is twofold: to demonstrate that the two-age construction exists in Paul's Christocentric eschatology and to identify the elements of man which belong historically to one age or the other. We shall see that the two-age construction as well as their identifying elements are implicit in Paul's eschatological structure. The point I want to make is that we should confront the reality of the two worlds that exist between the time of Christ's resurrection and His second coming. This chapter is essential for understanding the two-age construction as the necessary starting point for Christian apologetics. I will rely strongly upon the foundation of Vos, Ridderbos, and Gaffin as I develop this concept. I do not fail, however to consider other views concerning this construction.

Having verified and set forth the two-age construction, I focus the third chapter upon the antithesis of the two worlds and their comprehensive world and life view. The most precise description of the antithetical ages may be found in I Corinthians 1-3. This Pauline text describes for us the world and life view of the wisdom of the age to come as opposed to the wisdom of this present evil age. This distinction is imperative if we are going to understand the apologetic debate. I Corinthians 1-3 describes the distinctive antithetical position of the Christian over against his opponent.

At this point I discuss the significance of the two-age construction for Christian apologetics. I direct my attention in this closing chapter on the Reformed apologetic tradition, not only because of my own persuasion, which is evident throughout the work, but also because I believe the Reformed tradition has stood for a consistent and sincere biblical approach to apologetics. In the light of what has been said in the previous two chapters, I begin by showing that apologetics must follow eschatology in the encyclopedia of theological disciplines. With this established, I move on to consider the place which the two-age construction occupies in the apologetic spectrum. Our apologetic task is to defend the meaning of the age to come against the meaning of the present evil age. Reflecting on chapter one, I observe that Paul's theology is unique in that it is not synthetic, but that it is immersed totally in the sovereign revelation of God.

Chapter 1

BACKGROUND FOR DISCUSSING PAUL'S TWO-AGE CONSTRUCTION:
PLATO AND JEWISH APOCALYPTIC LITERATURE

PLATO

Throughout history many philosophers have spoken about two existing world orders. This concept is found in ancient Greek philosophy, as it is so eloquently formulated by Plato (427-347 B.C.). Though Plato was not the first to present such a concept, he developed it into a precise and popular formulation, one which has had a profound influence upon western philosophical thought and even on Christian thinking. In fact, I will discuss Plato's formulation because a synthesis has developed between Plato and Christianity throughout the history of the church. Christian theologians and philosophers throughout the ages have aligned or attempted to align themselves with the principles of Plato's two worlds.[1] This is evident in the philosophy and theology of the early church,[2] of the Middle Ages,[3] of the Renaissance,[4]

[1] Concerning such a synthesis, Herman Dooyeweerd, A New Critique of Theoretical Thought, trans. David H. Freeman & H. DeJongste, II (Philadelphia: The Presbyterian & Reformed Publishing Company, 1955), p. 9, refers to it as "Augustinian Platonic Scholasticism."

[2] Cornelius Van Til concentrates strongly upon the influence of Plato and Neoplatonic principles in the thought of the Apostolic Fathers, the Apologists, and early Augustine in his work A Christian Theory of Knowledge (n.p.: The Presbyterian & Reformed Publishing Company, 1969), pp. 72-147. Van Til does not mention Plato's concept of two worlds but one can see that it underlies much of the thought of the early church Fathers in Van Til's presentation.

[3] Plato's two worlds are also self-evident in what Paul Shorey, in Platonism: Ancient and Modern (Berkeley: University of California Press, 1938), pp. 91-117, calls the three chief lines of Platonic tradition in the Middle Ages: "1) the all pervading, often indirect, influence of the widely diffused later mystical and superstitious Neo-Platonism; 2) the controversy about the nature of general ideas of universals; 3) the impression on the medievil imagination of the story of creation as told in Chalcidius' Latin translation of the first half of the Timaeus." The initial point by Shorey has blossomed in the work of R. T. Wallis, Neo-Platonism (New York: Charles Scribner's Sons, 1972), p. 160.

[4] Whereas the late Middle Ages focused more upon Aristotle than Plato, the theology of the Renaissance turned from Aristotle

of the Cambridge Platonists,[5] and even of some modern evangelical scholars.[6] The question which I believe must arise is whether such a synthesis between Christianity and Plato is warranted. My task is to demonstrate that Plato's view of two worlds is antithetical to the Christian's view of two worlds as constructed by the Apostle Paul and that the history of Christian thought should never have synthesized Paul and Plato.

The Phaedo, the Republic, and the Timaeus, more than Plato's other works, present his formulation of the two existing world orders. In these works he also expounds his theory of ideas, which is not only the cornerstone of his thought but also the basis for any discussion of his two worlds.[7] One cannot

to Plato seeking to establish itself in the latter. The work of Marsilio Ficino, especially his Theologia Platonica, is a catalyst for this movement. He translated Plato into Latin and formed a club entitled the "Platonic Academy." Because of these activities of Ficino, Nicolas of Cusa is the first modern scholar to have full access to Plato's works. It is no accident, then, that in his work he posits two world orders in Platonic terms. Cf. Ernst Cassirer, The Platonic Renaissance in England, trans. James P. Pettegrove (New York: Thomas Nelson and Sons LTD, 1953), pp. 93,94. Also consult Shorey, op. cit., pp. 118-145.

[5]The cosmo-metaphysical conception of Plato's two worlds was accepted by Benjamin Whichcote (1609-1683), the leader of the Cambridge Platonists, as being a consistent biblical notion. Cf. C. A. Patrides, "'The High and Aiery Hills of Platonisme': An Introduction to The Cambridge Platonists," The Cambridge Platonists, ed. C. A. Patrides (Cambridge: Harvard University Press, 1970), pp. 1-41. On the Cambridge Platonists one should also consult James Deotis Roberts, From Puritanism to Platonism in Seventeenth Century England (Hague: Martinus Nijhoff, 1968).

[6]William G. T. Shedd provides an interesting introduction to C. Ackermann's work The Christian Element in Plato and the Platonic Philosophy, trans. Samuel Ralph Asbury (Edinburgh: T. & T. Clark, 1861), pp. 3,4. Shedd calls Ackermann's work "the best account that has yet been given of this very interesting phase of the philosophy of the Academy" (p. 3). Thus we find one of the most famous evangelical scholars of modern times not only advocating but also exalting classical synthesis. Shedd's introduction leads us to assume that he is in agreement with Ackermann's section "That which is Christian in Plato and His Philosophy" (pp. 231-251). In that section Ackermann is immersed in synthesis with Plato's two worlds.

[7]cf. Harold Cherniss, The Riddle of the Academy (New York: Russell and Russell, 1962), pp. 4,7.

comprehend Plato's two worlds unless he first penetrates Plato's theory of ideas. For this purpose, I shall direct our attention to the Timaeus, for it presents the many details of Plato's cosmology[8] and held a privileged status among the Christian theologians of the Middle Ages.[9]

In the Timaeus Plato's theory of ideas is not as pervasive as in the Phaedo, although he places that theory in the forefront of his cosmological discussion.[10] This balanced presentation which the Timaeus provides satisfies our immediate interest in his cosmo-metaphysical formulation of the two world orders and the place of the Demiurge in his thought.[11] These two existing world orders become evident as he begins with a distinction between what is "always real and has no becoming" and what is "always becoming and is never real."[12] The former is apprehended only by reason and can be expressed by definite statements because it is real and unchangeable. This ontological portion of Plato's theory of ideas maintains "that there is a world of permanent, unchanging and perfect entities which are unaffected by variations in circum-

[8]It is for this reason that Francis MacDonald Cornford entitles his translation and commentary on the Timeaus, Plato's Cosmology.

[9]In this chapter, as well as in the final chapter, both of these points are of particular importance to the concept of synthesis. Let it now be said that the importance of the Timaeus is a well-known fact concerning the theology of the Middle Ages. Cf. G. E. L. Owen, "The Place of the Timaeus in Plato's Dialogues," The Classical Quarterly, III (January-April, 1953), 79, and Richard Kroner, Speculation in Pre-Christian Philosophy (Philadelphia: The Westminster Press, 1956), p. 178.

[10]Sir William David Ross, Plato's Theory of Ideas (Oxford: At the Clarendon Press, 1951), p. 120.

[11]Also necessary to our discussion is the integral connection between Plato's two existing world orders and his conception of the Demiurge. The Demiurge is a vital part of Plato's cosmology. This is important because philosophers and theologians have attempted through history to identify Plato's Demiurge with the God of Christianity or to synthesize the two. We will be forced to investigate the validity of this parallel.

[12]Francis MacDonald Cornford, Plato's Cosmology: The 'Timaeus' of Plato Translated with a Running Commentary (New York: The Humanities Press, 1952), p. 22.

stances or conditions and which comprise reality."[13] In this higher world order, arguments of mathematics[14] and dialectic[15] bring forth a solid apprehension of truth and reality. This is the realm of Being, the eternal, intelligible, and the ideal world.[16]

[13] R. C. Cross and A. D. Woozley, "Knowledge, Belief, and the Forms," Plato: A Collection of Critical Essays, ed. Gregory Vlastos, I (Garden City: Doubleday and Company, Inc., 1971), 86.

[14] Plato's argument with the mathematicians of his day was that they had begun with mathematical hypotheses, and thus, in his estimation, they had failed to understand that mathematics must be a branch of knowledge proper, connected by dialectic to the conception of reality. Cf. R. M. Hare, "Plato and the Mathematicians," New Essays on Plato and Aristotle, ed. Renford Bambrough (London: Routledge and Kegan Paul, 1965), pp. 21-38. Anders Wedberg elaborates on this point in his work Plato's Philosophy of Mathematics (Stockholm: Almqvist and Wiksell, 1955), pp. 61,62. cf. also Nicholas P. White, Plato on Knowledge and Reality (Indianapolis: Hackett Publishing Company, 1976), pp. 96-99.

[15] According to the scholarly analysis of Francis MacDonald Cornford, Plato's Theory of Knowledge: The 'Theaetus' and the 'Sophist' of Plato Translated with a Running Commentary (London: Routledge and Kegan Paul LTD, 1935), p. 265, Plato's science of Dialectic studies "the structure of the real world of Forms." The objective of Plato's dialectic is clearly stated by Ross, op. cit., pp. 118-119: "The objective of [Plato's] dialectic is no longer to deduce all truth from a single transcendent truth. It is a more modest and a more realizable one---one with which Plato at least succeeds in making a beginning---that of tracing the relations of assertability and deniability that exist between Ideas, and the relations of genus and species that exist between them." For a dissertation on Plato's Dialectic cf. Julius Stenzel, Plato's Method of Dialectic, trans. and ed. D. J. Allan (Oxford: At the Clarendon Press, 1940), which is still a standard work in its field.

[16] Some Platonic scholars have chosen to refer to the ideal world (theory of ideas) as the world of forms. This is the position of Cross and Woozley, op. cit., pp. 81,82. They believe this grasps the meaning of eidos and idea better than the direct English transliteration of the Greek terms. They maintain that the exact English transliteration renders an unfortunate misunderstanding of Plato's use of the concept. The English connotation tends to lead us to believe ideas exist only in the mind and are only "subjective." According to Plato nothing could be more false. For example, the real unchanging idea of Beauty is independent of any idea of our subjective conception of Beauty. Rather, Beauty itself is truly real and the object of knowledge. Though in this work we will remain in the popular tradition of

On the other hand, there is the realm of Becoming which is the world perceived by our senses.[17] As far as Plato is concerned, one perceives a thing which has become, and yet, that thing passes away or perishes.[18] The world of things perceived are not constant; it is not the world of truth and reality. Sense perception is, therefore, irrational and not dependable. Plato states that there are several ways in which sense perception is irrational. In support of this he offers the example of measuring the width of the sun. When one looks at the sun, it seems to be about one foot in width. Therefore, an assertion on the basis of sense perception that the sun is larger than the earth would not be valid, since mathematics would prove otherwise. Thus, in distinction from mathematics and dialectic, the visible world (the object of physics) belongs to a lower order of existence, and because it is always changing it has no real being. Therefore, Plato calls the cosmos the realm of Becoming.

Concerning the cosmos, Plato asks the following question: "Has it always been, without any source of becoming; or has it come to be, starting from some beginning?"[19] Plato states that it has come to be, because all things of the cosmos are sensible things and because all sensible things are things which become and can be generated. He observes that everything which becomes must have a cause. In his words, it must have a maker and father. He also observes that the maker modeled the cosmos after one of two patterns: after that which is in an unchanging state or after that which has come to be (always changing). According to Plato, the world was fashioned after the eternal world but is a changing image or likeness of the eternal model. It follows from this that for Plato there

using the ideal world (theory of ideas), we must, nevertheless, know exactly how Plato employed his theory. Ideas should never be understood as subjective; they are objects of knowledge rather then products of a person's mind.

[17]It is important for us to keep in mind that the world of Platonic ideas has a separate existence from the world of matter. In defense of this cf. Harold Cherniss, *Aristotle's Criticism of Plato and the Academy*, I (Baltimore: The John Hopkins Press, 1944), pp. 206-211. For a thorough discussion of the relationship between idea and matter, cf. pp. 174-478.

[18]Cross and Woozley, op. cit., pp. 76-81.

[19]Cornford, *Plato's Cosmology: The 'Timaeus' of Plato*, p. 22.

can never be a final statement of exact truth within the changing cosmos.[20] Truth is relative. Plato's *a priori* epistemology is rooted in and cannot be separated from his concept of ontology, that is, the universal, real, and unchangeable world of Forms.[21]

It should be observed that the words "starting" and "beginning" in Plato's discussion of the cosmos have caught the attention of many Christian theologians and philosophers throughout the centuries.[22] His position has led many of them to believe that Plato was setting forth a theory of creation which corresponds to the Christian view of creation.[23] Such a connection with Christian theism, however, is untenable. The words "beginning" and "starting," with reference to the visible world, are better translated "principle."[24] According to Plato, the philosophical issue does not center on a theory of creation in which the visible world had its first moment; instead the issue centers on whether the physical universe should be classified under Being or Becoming. Plato believed that the world should be classified under Becoming: "It has become for it is both visible and tangible, and corporeal; all such things are sensible, and sensible objects, apprehended by opinion with sensation, are obviously objects of becoming and birth."[25] As one can see, the issue is not the creating of the world *ex*

[20]This point is clearly brought out by Cornford, ibid., pp. 23-24. He writes: "The chief point established in this prelude is that the visible world, of which an account is to be given, is a changing image or likeness (*eikon*) of an eternal model. It is a realm, not of being, but of becoming. The inference is that no account that we or anyone else can give of it will ever be more than 'likely'. There can never be a final statement of exact truth about this changing object."

[21]Cross and Woozley clearly attest to this, op. cit., pp. 89-95. Frederick Copleston, A History of Philosophy, Vol. I, i, Greece and Rome (Garden City: Image Books, 1962), pp. 166-167, also realizes this connection in Plato's thought.

[22]cf. Gordon H. Clark, Thales to Dewey: A History of Philosophy (Boston: Houghton Mifflin Company, 1957), pp. 93,94.

[23]For example, Richard Kroner, op. cit., p. 167, believes that Plato's speculative philosophy as well as his divine architect which forms the universe anticipated biblical revelation.

[24]This point concerning translation is made by Gordon H. Clark, op. cit., p. 93.

[25]Ibid. Clark's interpretation can be affirmed also in Plato's concept of eternity as it is presented by Cherniss, Aristotle's Criticism of Plato and the Academy, I, p. 212.

nihilo; the issue is that the world (realm of becoming) has become by its maker or cause (Dimiurge).[26] This makes it important that we investigate the relationship of the Demiurge to the two existing world orders.

Plato was convinced that the visible world is the product of a divinely intelligent maker who was aiming at that which is good. The logical pattern is as follows: since the visible world is good, its Maker must have copied a model which is eternal, i.e. the Absolute Good.[27] Thus the visible world is nothing more than a copy or image of the real or Ideal world. All of this means that according to Plato the Demiurge is an independent mediator between Form and Matter.[28] Throughout the history of philosophy the question which arises at this point is this: if the Demiurge mediates between Form and Matter, how can it operate independently? Or, to put it another way, since the Demiurge is independent, why did it make any world at all? Gordon Clark provides insight in answering this question.

> ...the problem for Plato is at least superficially easy. In addition to the world of Ideas as an eternally existing reality that can serve as a model for a physical universe, the Maker, or Demiurge, also an independent and eternal existence, is confronted with another independent principle: chaotic matter. Plato therefore proposes a world-view with three eternal and independent principles. These may not be all equally supreme, for the Ideas are highest, the Demiurge is second, and matter is lowest. But though not all equally supreme, they are

[26] As Ross, op. cit., pp. 128, 137, points out: "Thus the Timaeus is deistic rather than pantheistic in its theology. At the same time, the Demiourgos is not viewed as omnipotent, nor as creating the world out of nothing...the Demiourgos turns the world of random events into the ordered world as it is." Paul Shorey, Platonism: Ancient and Modern, pp. 29-31, defends the view that Plato was not a pantheist, although pantheism occupies an exalted place in the history of Platonism.

[27] Cornford, Plato's Cosmology: The 'Timaeus' of Plato, p. 28.

[28] With respect to the independence of the Demiurge and Form, Ross, op. cit., p. 127, writes: "There is no foundation, anywhere in Plato, for the view that the Demiourgos is to be identified with the Form of good, or with the Forms taken as a whole. Nor does the Demiourgos make the Forms. They are present from the start as models to which he looks in making what he does make, the world as we find it."

independent: no one of them is the cause of the other. Now, if the existence of chaotic matter be granted as a principle or brute fact without an explanation, then Plato's answer to the question, why God made a world, is easy and adequate. God was good and free from envy; he wished to bring the chaotic matter to as high a degree of perfection as possible; therefore, using the Ideas as a model or blueprint, he fashioned the matter into a beautiful physical universe.[29]

From this explanation one can see that the place of supremacy belongs to the Idea, and not to the Demiurge or to Matter. Nevertheless, both the Demiurge and Matter are important to Plato's three-part structure. The Demiurge becomes the focus of attention if we examine the rational ordering of the universe as a process of creation in time. It is interesting to note that within this context the Demiurge is connected with the concept of "myth" or "story" (<u>mythos</u>). (Plato wants us to understand that the Demiurge is a mythical figure who stands for something which is seriously meant. What does he stand for? He stands for a divine Reason working for good ends [30]).

According to Cornford, it is at this point that the purpose of the <u>Timaeus</u> emerges. That purpose is to instruct us about the universe as the operation of divine Reason.[31] The universe is not aimless chaos: instead, it has order because the Demiurge which formed

[29]Clark, op. cit., p. 94. In distinction from Clark, Ross, op. cit., p. 127, states there are four eternal and independent principles in Plato's world-views: "These four are the world of Forms, the Demiourgos, space, and random events in space."

[30]cf. Cornford, <u>Plato's Cosmology</u>: <u>The 'Timaeus' of Plato</u>, p. 38. "We can hardly avoid drawing the conclusion" comments R. Hackforth in his article "Plato's Theism," <u>Studies in Plato's Metaphysics</u>, ed. R. E. Allen (New York: The Humanities Press, 1965), p. 439, "that (a) the Demiurge is to be identified with <u>nous</u>, i.e. he is the 'mythical' equivalent of <u>nous</u>, (b) <u>nous</u> is a more ultimate principle than the <u>phyche tou kosmou</u>. Hackforth continues: "Reason then, as well as soul, is found in the Universe and is due to the action of God, who is himself identified with Reason. In other words, the Universe is rational and good in so far as God's rational nature and goodness are imported to it; it is irrational and bad in so far as God's rational nature and goodness are not wholly imported to it." (p. 444)

[31]Cornford, <u>Plato's Cosmology</u>: <u>The 'Timaeus' of Plato</u>, p. 38.

it is the mythical representation of the divine Reason. One must realize that in the Timaeus, as well as in the other writings of Plato, ambiguity surrounds the concept of divine Reason.[32] Plato does not give us a precise view of it, but forces us to focus upon its mythical representative, the Demiurge.

Plato's cosmology is also mythical, for it comes to us in the form of a cosmogony, a "story" of events spread out in time.[33] This mythical cosmology enters Greek philosophy in distinct contrast to earlier cosmogonies of both an evolutionary type and an Atomistic type.[34] Plato describes the universe to his readers by imagining its construction by the Demiurge and making it grow rationally before their own eyes. Even though the universe is a product of rational construction we must remember that according to Plato the universe is a changing object and can never be identified as exact truth. The universe must always remain in the realm of "becoming" and within the framework of cosmogony, if we are to interpret Plato's philosophy accurately.

As we have mentioned earlier, some thinkers have synthesized Christian theism with Plato's god, the Demiurge. Certain points must be noted before such an alleged correspondence can be affirmed. First as we have stated, the Demiurge is a mythical entity which stands for divine Reason. This means that we must be careful to identify what we are synthesizing with Christian theism: is it the Demiurge, or is it divine Reason? Throughout the history of theology and philosophy, each has found a number of supporters. But the problem in dealing with the Demiurge and divine Reason is to demonstrate, without any doubt, that Plato viewed both as real and personal. Not only would supporters have to demonstrate this reality and personal quality, but they would also have to show that Plato viewed either of these concepts as in some way superior to the Ideal. Taking Plato's philosophy as a whole, I believe that all such demon-

[32]This ambiguity permeates Copleston's discussion of Plato's doctrine of Forms, op. cit., pp. 202-218.
[33]Cornford, Plato's Cosmology: The 'Timaeus' of Plato.
[34]According to Cornford (Plato's Cosmology: The 'Timaeus' of Plato, p. 31), the evolutionary type suggested a "birth and growth of the world, due to some spontaneous force of life in Nature", whereas the Atomistic type suggested a birth and growth of the world by a "blind and undesigned collision of lifeless atoms".

strations would be forced.35 One would have to isolate abstractly certain attributes or characteristics of Plato's god, change their meaning as they appear in the holistic structure of Plato's philosophy, then synthesize these attributes or characteristics with Christian theism. Not only does such a procedure destroy the distinctiveness of Christian theism, but it also destroys Plato's view of his own god. Such an adventure is an injustice both to Christian thought and to Platonic thought. We must underline, therefore, that Plato's formulation of god is not a faithful response to the revelation of the Christian God, but rather a rejection of Him.

In the second place, it is a mistake to think Plato was a monotheist or that the Demiurge was for him an object of worship. Nowhere is either of these ideas conveyed in Plato's writings. More strikingly, the Demiurge is not even pictured as a religious figure. Plato believed that both the world and heavenly bodies are divine.36 In fact, in the Epinomis, he speaks about a cult of celestial gods. In short, Plato's writings are permeated with polytheism, not monotheism. It should be clear, therefore, that Plato's Demiurge cannot be aligned with the God of Christianity because his Demiurge is not a monotheistic object of worship and the supreme figure of religion.37

In the third place, we should not give the Demiurge the status of omnipotent Creator. According to Plato, the Demiurge operates upon materials which

 35Copleston, op. cit., p. 216, also sees very serious difficulties with such a synthesis. This can also be seen in a careful examination of Glen R. Marrow's article "Necessity and Persuasion in Plato's 'Timaeus'," Studies in Plato's Metaphysics, ed. R. E. Allen (New York: The Humanities Press, 1965), pp. 421-437, and Gregory Vlastos' article "Creation in the 'Timaeus': Is it a Fiction?" Studies in Plato's Metaphysics, ed. R. E. Allen (New York: The Humanities Press, 1965), pp. 401-419.
 36cf. R. Hackforth, op. cit., p. 440.
 37Cornford, Plato's Cosmology: The 'Timaeus' of Plato, p. 35, makes a relevant remark: "It is not fair either to Plato or the New Testament to ascribe the most characteristic revelations of the Founder of Christianity to a pagan polytheist". As far as the realm of theism is concerned, Plato's Demiurge does not have an independent existence (cf. Hackforth, op. cit., pp. 440-443).

he has not created.[38] The Demiurge is confronted with "all that is visible," in which chaos and disorderly motion are prevalent. He is not responsible for this disorder; instead, he will introduce order "so far as he can" into the world of becoming. If we go one step further, we realize it is also incorrect to assume that the Demiurge creates the world of Becoming in which the images of the Forms are mirrored.[39] This would be impossible, according to Plato, since the Forms are eternally real and self-existing. How could the Demiurge create that which has eternally been? The function of the Demiurge is to bring order as far as he can to the realm of Becoming. This in itself indicates that the Demiurge is not omnipotent. Besides this, in the second part of the discourse of the Timaeus, Plato makes very clear that the Demiurge is not even the sole cause of Becoming. There are also secondary causes at work. These secondary causes, the eternal state of Matter, the supreme and eternal state of the Form, and the limited operation of the Demiurge eliminate omnipotence as a characteristic of Plato's god.[40] Very clearly, then, the Demiurge is not the omnipotent Creator God of Christian theism.

One last topic remains for us to observe very briefly in regard to Plato's world order: ethics.[41] Plato conceived the world as being rationally ordered

[38] As Marrow, op. cit., p. 425, writes: "But like any other craftsman, the cosmic demiurge uses materials fire, water, air, earth; and these materials and their natures are obviously an important factor in determining what kind of product he can fashion from them...these materials and their inherent powers are the auxiliary causes with which the demiurge works and whose co-operation with him he has to effect," or as R. Hackforth, op. cit., p. 439, pointedly writes: "In the Timaeus the Demiurge...brings order into unordered chaos..."

[39] Cornford, Plato's Cosmology: The 'Timaeus' of Plato, p. 37.

[40] For further critical insight into this discussion, cf. M. B. Foster, "Christian Theology and Modern Science of Nature (Part One)," Mind, XLIV (1935), 466, and M. B. Foster, "Christian Theology and Modern Science of Nature (Part Two)," Mind, XLV (1936), 6.

[41] The foundation of Plato's ethical thought can be drawn from Socratic ideas, though there are some notable differences. One should consult John Gould, The Development of Plato's Ethics (New York: Russell and Russell, 1972), pp. 3-67 and Terence Irwin, Plato's Moral Theory: The Early and Middle Dialogues (Oxford: Clarendon Press, 1977), pp. 13-176.

after the Form of Absolute Good. His ethic is, therefore, directed towards the attainment of man's highest good.[42] This comes to expression in the fact that man's life is the pursuit of virtue, which is the attainment of happiness and goodness. In this context man should become like god, who represents the supremacy of the law.[43] However, what happens when man does express evil? Although man does express evil, Plato believes that he does it unknowingly and unwillingly.

Even though there is much more we could say concerning Plato's ethics, it is sufficient to highlight some important points: 1) the universe (i.e., the world of matter) is good, 2) man is created good in the universe, 3) man's life is the pursuit of virtue (happiness and goodness), 4) any evil in man comes to expression unconsciously, and 5) there is not an adequate distinction between god and man in the attainment of virtue.

In this section we have briefly discussed Plato's idea of two existing world orders. We have also seen the place of the Demiurge and have briefly commented upon his ethics in relationship to his world orders. Against this background we raise two questions. How is Paul's two-age construction antithetical to Plato's view? How does Paul's two-age construction provide the Christian with a defense against Plato? We will attempt to answer these questions after we investigate Paul's two-age construction.

JEWISH APOCALYPTIC LITERATURE

In the previous section we mentioned the attempt in the history of Christian theology and philosophy to synthesize the philosophy of Plato with Pauline

---

[42] This concept is definitely rooted in Socrates. Gould, op. cit., p. 49, comments concerning Socrates that "the end of every action is our real happiness, and we act, not at random, but because in each instance we feel it better to act in one way rather than another."

[43] Gould, op. cit., p. 99, writes: "The whole message of the Laws is contained in the phrase 'assimilation to god' (homoiōsis theōi), and in the final rejection of 'Protagoras' relativism, Plato asserts that god, not man, is the measure of all things."

theology and to label that synthesis Christian orthodoxy. We were careful to note that it was Christian theologians and philosophers who did the synthesizing. In this section, however, we are confronted with a different kind of synthesis: the synthesis of the apocalyptic literature and New Testament literature. Some scholars believe that the writers of the New Testament (e.g. Paul) synthesized the content of apocalyptic literature with their own interpretation of the life of Christ or life in Christ. The question which I wish to address is whether Paul actually effected such a synthesis.

Since the appearance of the critical article Die jüdische Apokalyptik in ihrer geschichtlichen Entwicklung ("Jewish Apocalyptic in its Historical Development"), written by Adolf Hilgenfeld in 1857, Biblical and apocalyptic scholars have tried to determine how the apocalyptic literature has affected New Testament theology. Ernst Käsemann's viewpoint is presently popular. He alleges that the "apocalyptic was the mother of all Christian theology."[44] Käsemann uses the term "mother" to suggest that all Christian theology is determined by the apocalyptic. This, of course, includes Paul's theology--our immediate interest. We must realize, however, that Käsemann saw the Easter "event" and the outpouring of the Holy Spirit as initiating a new apocalyptic in the primitive Christian community.[45] As far as Käsemann is concerned, these two "events," however, do not essentially change the content of the old apocalyptic (pre-Christian) literature; rather these "events" serve to illuminate the older apocalyptic as well as to fulfill it. One can see from this that Käsemann does

[44] New Testament Questions of Today, trans. W. J. Montague (London: SCM Press LTD, 1969), p. 102. This position is explained in Richard J. Bauckham's article "The Rise of Apocalyptic," Themelios, III (January, 1978), 10: "more and more apocalyptic must be seen as a crucial historical bridge between the testaments". This view is defended by D. S. Russell, The Method and Message of Jewish Apocalyptic: 200 B.C.-A.D. 100 (Philadelphia: The Westminster Press, 1964), p. 34, and Wolfgang Roth, "Between Tradition and Expectation: The Origin and Role of Biblical Apocalyptic," Explor IV (Spring, 1978), 13. For details concerning the connection between Hilgenfeld and Käsemann cf. Walter Schmithals, The Apocalyptic Movement: Introduction and Interpretation, trans. John E. Steely (Nashville: Abingdon Press, 1975), pp. 54,65. It should also be noted that "Christian theology" refers here to the traditional New Testament canon.

[45] cf. Käsemann, op. cit., pp. 101-102.

not view his critical task as synthesizing apocalyptic literature and Christian theology. Instead he sees himself as critically unveiling the true roots of Christian theology as it appears in the traditional New Testament canon. Since not all scholars agree with Käsemann, we do well to ask whether his position is justified. Let us focus upon the Apostle Paul in answering this question.

To begin with, we must admit that much of the eschatological terminology found in Paul is also clearly found in the apocalyptic literature.[46] It is also true that much of this similar terminology is lacking from the traditional Old Testament Canon.[47] This does not mean, however, that the theological substance of Paul's terminology is identical or even closely similar to that of the apocalyptic writers.[48] Nor does it mean that Paul's eschatological terminology opposes or contradicts the eschatological framework of Old Testament theology. The similarity in terminology can be explained by understanding that there is a historical continuity between apocalyptic literature and Christianity.[49] Paul's education would undoubtly have made him familiar with the eschatological terminology of the apocalyptic. As Geerhardus Vos

[46] Geerhardus Vos, The Pauline Eschatology (Grand Rapids: Wm. B. Eerdmans Publishing Company, 1972), pp. 22-29.

[47] As Leon Morris, Apocalyptic (Grand Rapids: Wm. B. Eerdmans Publishing Company, 1972), p. 73, writes: "The Christian movement has its affinities with the apocalyptic movement. The language of the apocalyptists has influenced that of the Christians. The characteristic expressions of the Gospels often seem to receive more emphasis in apocalyptic than they do, for example, in the Old Testament." Morris realizes, however, that the theological substance in the language is not the same (cf. pp. 73, 74).

[48] We believe Gerhard Ebeling, "The Ground of Christian Theology," Journal for Theology and the Church, no. 6, Apocalypticism, ed. Robert W. Funk (New York: Herder and Herder, 1969), pp. 52,53, speaks to the point when he says that the New Testament is "not apocalyptic systems of ideas, but individual sayings with an apocalyptic background; not a disclosure of apocalyptic mysteries, but concrete, apocalyptically grounded instructions for the present, not a code language of dreams and visions, but one that is universally understandable, not a prophetic authority that is borrowed under a pseudonym, but one that is exercised in personal responsibility".

[49] The critical scholar Walter Schmithals, op. cit., pp. 170-171 points this out.

points out, "there is no escape from the conclusion that a piece of Jewish theology has been here by Revelation incorporated into the Apostle's teaching. The main structure of the Jewish apocalyptic is embodied in our Lord's teaching as well as in Paul's."[50] Although this is true, it does not mean that there is a <u>substantive</u> identity between the eschatological terminology.[51]

I believe that if one thoroughly examines the content of Paul's eschatology, the fundamental differences will emerge. One such difference is that Paul's eschatological conception of the Messianic Kingdom of God is not of the political, national, earthly, provisional kingdom which is found in the apocalyptic literature. Instead, the death and resurrection of Jesus Christ is the focal point of a historical, ethical, and religious kingdom.[52] Again, in regard to substance, the eschatology of the apocalyptic literature is inconsistent and confusing, whereas Paul's

[50]Geerhardus Vos, op. cit., p. 28n. It should be noted that the term "structure" does not mean "substance" here. I believe that Vos' statement correctly indicates that if there is any theological similarity between the apocalyptic and Paul, it is not because Paul was a synthesizer but rather because they both had certain roots in Old Testament revelation. Cf. also J. Gresham Machen, <u>The Origin of Paul's Religion</u> (Grand Rapids: Wm. B. Eerdmans Publishing Company, 1925), pp. 180-194. With respect to Paul, however, Machen, is also very clear to point out that "Paulinism is based not upon later developments [apocalyptic literature] but upon the religion of the Prophets and the Psalms" (p. 180).

[51]Walter Schmithals, op. cit., p. 171, points this out in his understanding of the substantive differences: "With respect to the <u>substantive</u> relationship, however, this assertion [apocalyptic was the mother of Christian theology] is by no means correct. For in substance the New Testament understanding of existence stands in sharp tension with the apocalyptic view of reality and relatively close to the original Old Testament declaration of the relationship of God, world, and man." This point is defended also by W. D. Davies, <u>Paul and Rabbinic Judaism: Some Rabbinic Elements in Pauline Theology</u> (London: SPCK, 1965), p. 290, and Hans Conzelmann, <u>A Commentary on the First Epistle to the Corinthians</u>, ed. George W. MacRae, S. J., trans. James W. Leitch (Philadelphia: Fortress Press, 1975), p. 43.

[52]Vos, op. cit., p. 28n, writes: "...there is no place in the Apostle's (Paul) scheme for an earthly, provisional kingdom of the Messiah. Paul's polemic against heathenism is of a strictly religious nature".

is relatively simple and consistent.[53] These basic characteristics point to the fact that the substance of Paul's eschatology is not determined by the apocalyptic literature, but is antithetical to it. The writings of Paul demonstrate complete submission to the sovereign redemptive-historical plan of God as it unfolds in the pattern of creation, fall, and redemption. The fulfillment of the eschatological vision fails in the apocalyptic literature because it loses sight of this progressive redemptive-historical plan of God.

I believe it is fair to conclude that the issue is not to place the substance of the apocalyptic literature into the "Easter event" and the "event of Pentecost" as Käsemann has done, but to see how the death and resurrection of Jesus Christ and the coming of the Holy Spirit provided Paul with a metamorphic formulation against the background of the apocalyptic literature. The so-called objectivity of Käsemann fails to penetrate Paul's thought at this crucial point. Käsemann's view also fails to recognize that the continuity of terminology provides Paul with an apologetic point of contact. The meaning of Paul's terminology, however, is grounded in the process of redemptive-historical revelation, which is antithetical to the ambiguous and inconsistent substance of apocalyptic terminology.

Thus far we have merely asserted that there is an antithesis between the content of Pauline theology and the content of the apocalyptic literature. This will now be demonstrated by turning to the eschatological framework of the apocalyptic literature with a special reference to the two-ages.

According to most scholars, apocalyptic literature appears in the world of Semetic-speaking Israel and Jewish Christianity between 200 B. C. and A. D. 100.[54] The word apocalyptic is derived from the Greek work <u>apokalypsis</u>, which means "unveiling" or "uncovering." It has the same meaning as its Latin equivalent, "revelation", and thus, signifies the disclosure of some hidden truth, particularly about God and His divine plan.[55] These hidden truths are associated with the Jews who lived in dispersion during the inter-

[53]Ibid.
[54]Russell, op. cit., p. 15, and Leon Morris, Op. cit., p. 19.
[55]Russell, op. cit., p. 36.

testamental period as well as with those who remained in Palestine. The Jewish people were living in despair, looking to the apocalyptists for a vision of hope. W. O. E. Oesterley says, "in this world of despair hope is the main underlying motive-power which prompted the writers of the Apocalypses".[56] Since this is a fair observation, S. B. Frost is correct when he states that the "apocalyptic possesses a very definite Sitz im Leben".[57] The specific content of the literature could never have arisen apart from the historical circumstances of the Jewish people.[58] The Jews saw themselves surrounded by a world of evil and hopelessness. The Apocalyptists (and thus the Jewish people), therefore, envisioned destruction for the world and found their hope in the world to come (a new world), where the righteous would receive the blessings and prosperity of God and where evildoers would be turned away by judgment. The Sitz im Leben is relevent at this point. Oesterley points out that the Apocraphal books "are only made with a view to comforting the oppressed and afflicted with the thought that even the most mighty of earthly powers are shortly to be overthrown by the advent of the new and glorious era when every injustice and all the incongruities of life will be done away with."[59] We note, therefore that the Apocalyptist sees his historical situation as the point from which to view the future. This perspective leads us to realize that apocalyptic literature is almost exclusively concerned with the future;

[56]R. H. Charles, The Book of Enoch, Intro. W. O. E. Oesterley (London: Society for Promoting Christian Knowledge, 1917), p. viii. cf. Morris, op. cit., pp. 37-39.

[57]Old Testament Apocalyptic: Its Origins and Growth (London: The Epworth Press, 1952), p. 4. In endorsing the term "Sitz im Leben," we are not accepting all of its critical nuances; we are merely admitting that the apocalyptic arises out of a particular historical situation in Hebraic existence.

[58]Geerhardus Vos, "Review: W. O. E. Oesterley's, The Books of the Apocrypha," Princeton Theological Review XIV (1916), 136, agrees with this point. It should also be noted that the Apocryphal books themselves reflect this historical situation. cf. R. K. Harrison, Introduction to the Old Testament (Grand Rapids: Wm. B. Eerdmans Publishing Company, 1969), p. 1175. It is not our concern to go into detail about the historical situation of the Jewish people in this period. For this one can consult D. S. Russell, op. cit., pp. 15-33, and R. K. Harrison, op. cit., pp. 1175-1193.

[59]Charles, op. cit., p. ix. cf. Morris, op. cit., pp. 39-41.

it is eschatological.60

There is another factor which emerges as one studies the apocalyptic literature, namely, the appearance of frequent inconsistencies and contradictions of thought. Charles pointed out that one of the main reasons these inconsistencies and contradictions existed among the Apocalyptists was because their minds "were saturated with the traditional thoughts and ideas of the Old Testament, and, on the other hand, they were eagerly absorbing the newer conceptions which the spirit of the age had brought into being."61 The attempt of various authors to harmonize these two ideas was not always successful, and therefore it is not surprising to find illogical and contradictory material. This illogical and contradictory material is evident in a study of the eschatological content of the apocalyptic literature. Its eschatological message, which derives from the idea of the two worlds, is anything but systematic.62 The Jew who lived at the time of Christ, or even in the latter part of the first century A. D., did not have one uniform opinion of the future presented to him in

60As C. K. Barrett, "New Testament Eschatology," Scottish Journal of Theology VI (1952), 140, writes: "The basic principle upon which their apocalyptists thought rests is that of the Two Ages, the present Age in which the powers of wickedness are in revolt against God and cause trouble and grief, especially for the elect, and the Age to Come, in which God will assert His authority, judge, and punish the wicked and reign over His saints in bliss". Morris, op. cit., p. 11, states: "For the apocalyptist the whole of history pointed to the End and he concentrated his gaze on it". Consult also Rudolf Bultmann, "History and Eschatology in the New Testament," New Testament Studies, I (1954-1955), p. 7.

61Charles, op. cit., p. x.

62The consensus of scholarly opinion has been that the eschatological message of the apocalyptic has its roots in what orthodox Christianity would call the Old Testament prophetical canon. Some scholars go on to conclude that pagan influences and the historical situation in the intertestamental period distorted the message of prophetic eschatology and that this led to various inconsistent conceptions. One should consult the recent works of Richard J. Bauckham, op. cit., pp. 10-18; Morris, op. cit., pp. 42,43; Paul D. Hanson, The Dawn of Apocalyptic (Philadelphia: Fortress Press, 1975) and Otto Plöger, Theocracy and Eschatology, trans. S. Rudman (Oxford: Basil Blackwell, 1968), pp. 26-105.

the apocalyptic.⁶³ The opinions were almost as various as the writers themselves. Let us look at a few of these opinions.

In examining *The Psalms of Solomon*, historical scholarship immediately directs our attention to the famous Messianic psalm found in chapter seventeen. This psalm presents the Messiah as a powerful, militant king who will come and destroy the unrighteous rulers of the world and who will deliver Jerusalem from its gentile oppressors. By the very word of his mouth he will destroy all godless nations (17. 24-27). He is described as a descendant of the line of David (17.23), who will gather his people together and rule them in righteousness (17.28-30). He will divide the land of Israel among his holy people, admitting no foreigners. The heathen nations will serve the righteous (17.30-32), coming to seek the glory of the Messiah by bringing exiled Jews as their gifts (17.34-36).

The Psalms of Solomon clearly conceives the Messianic kingdom in Jewish national terms (the kingdom is confined to the earth, and its center is Jerusalem). There is no mention of a future supernatural kingdom. The psalm focuses upon Israel's freedom from its enemies and also upon a consequent state of blessedness here on earth. In this kingdom the purpose of the gentiles will be to serve the Jews. From the statement in 17.30-32 that foreigners shall never again dwell in Palestine, it maybe deduced that this earthly kingdom will be eternal and that the Messiah will smite the earth by the word of his mouth (17.31,39).⁶⁴

In this psalm, one sees a vision or notion of two worlds: a present earthly gentile kingdom and a future dominant Hebrew kingdom. It is apparent

⁶³This point is brought out by Frost, op. cit., p. 21 and Herman Ridderbos, *The Coming of the Kingdom*, trans. H. de Jongste (Philadelphia: The Presbyterian and Reformed Publishing Company, 1969), p. 10.

⁶⁴These conclusions concerning the messianic kingdom presented in *The Psalms of Solomon* has been affirmed by important scholars: cf. D. S. Russell, op. cit., p. 289; H. Ridderbos, op. cit., p. 10; R. H. Charles, *A Critical History of the Doctrine of a Future Life* (London: Adam and Charles Black, 1913), p. 270; and H. H. Rowley, *The Relevance of Apocalyptic: A Study of Jewish and Christian Apocalypses from Daniel to the Revelation* (London: Lutterworth Press, 1963), p. 79.

that the psalm forces the Old Testament concepts of the Messiah, of righteousness, the line of David, judgment, and gentiles to conform with the historical situation of Hebraic nationalism. These Old Testament concepts are thus defiled by nationalistic sentiment.

This psalm, therefore, is not part of an organic process of revelation beginning with the Old Testament and continuing to the Apostle Paul. Rather it is steeped in its own Sitz im Leben without remaining within the organic process of revelation.

In The Testament of the Twelve Patriarchs, the eschatological picture is different. Instead of painting a national picture, this pseudepigraphic writing presents a supernatural cosmic picture: "the coming messianic kingdom will entail the redemption of the whole cosmos, the resurrection of the dead, the universal judgment of the whole world and eternal life in God's paradise."[65] There is no doubt that the Messianic kingdom presented here is everlasting, but scholars disagree as to whether it is an earthly or heavenly kingdom. The point I want to make here, however, is that the kingdoms presented in the Twelve Patriarchs and The Psalms of Solomon differ in that the former is cosmic whereas the latter is national. Here lies a clear example of the inconsistent eschatological picture of the apocalyptic literature.

Parts of the Book of Enoch and of the Assumption of Moses present the future kingdom as a heavenly world rather than an earthly messianic reign. We must also note the complicated picture presented in the Similitudes of Enoch (I Enoch 37-71). In the Similitudes, the coming of the future kingdom will coincide with the coming of the Son of Man,[66] who will ascend to the throne of glory where He will exercise judgment (45.3; 48.2f.; 49.4; 61.8ff). At that time

[65] Ridderbos, op. cit., p. 10.
[66] Though the term Son of Man is the same one used in Daniel 7, the Son of Man presented in the Similitudes is not the Messianic Son of Man presented in Daniel (Christ). Nevertheless, the Son of Man presented in the Similitudes is an apocalyptic conception of the Messiah, although it is not the Messiah revealed in the New Testament. Machen clearly makes this point, op. cit., pp. 186-189. This is also brought out by H. H. Rowley, op. cit., p. 61, and D. S. Russell, op. cit., p. 327.

the dead will be raised and will appear before the Son of man for judgment with angels and earthly kings (51.1ff; 54.1ff; 61.5,8). The sinners and the godless will then be driven off the face of the earth (38.3; 41.2; 45.6; 53.1ff; 54.1ff), and at this time God will transform both heaven and earth, making them a place of blessedness (45.4-5). Thus, the kingdom presented in the Similitudes is universal in its scope and everlasting in its endurance.

A complication concerning the setting of this kingdom enters the discussion at this point: the picture of a transformed heaven and earth (45.4-5). Such imagery is not found in apocalyptic literature previous to the Similitudes. D. S. Russell points out that "the context of this passage indicates that the throne of the Son of Man is to be set up on earth where his elect dwell (52.4; 45.4), ...while on the other hand, the elect are to dwell with the Elect One (Son of Man--61.4), whose dwelling-place is with the Lord of Spirits in prison (49.2)"[67] What is to be made of this obscure dual character of the Kingdom? S. Mowinckel may be correct when he tells us that the answer "is inherent in the nature of the subject," that is in the "super-terrestrial logic of the Kingdom" of the author's vision.[68] Thus, the elect of God will inhabit both a transformed kingdom on earth and in heaven. This eschatological dualism has no correspondence with the empirical world.

The Assumption of Moses does not present the forementioned picture of the kingdom. Instead, the Assumption of Moses pictures the future estate of the kingdom to be in heaven, not a kingdom on earth. It is also interesting to note that in the Assumption of Moses God Himself, not a Messiah will sit upon His throne while the whole earth trembles (10.3-4). God will punish the gentiles and will destroy their idols (10.7). The angels of God will exercise His judgment upon His enemies (10.2), and Satan will be utterly consumed (10.1). In those days the mourning of Israel will cease and she will be exalted into heaven while her enemies will suffer in Gehenna (10.9-10).

The authors of the Similitudes and the Assumption of Moses abandoned the idea that the Messianic kingdom

---

[67]op. cit., p. 290.
[68]Sigmund Mowinckel, He That Cometh, trans. G. W. Anderson (Oxford: Basil Blackwell, 1956), p. 406.

is coming to the earth because their Sitz im Leben has rendered the earth totally unfit for the establishment of such a kingdom. In their view only a transformed earth and a new heaven could be places of eternal bliss. Even in this setting, however, the messiah whom they picture is not the Messiah of the New Testament. The recognition of this point has proved to be a key argument against Käsemann's view. If the Messiah of the New Testament is shaped by the Messiah presented by the authors of apocalyptic literature, then certain fundamental aspects ought to be apparent in their writings: e.g. the activity of the Messiah in creation, the personal salvific union between Christ and the believer, and the deity of the Messiah.[69] But these aspects are not apparent in their writings. Leon Morris,[70] and Wayne G. Rollins[71] have pointed to this glaring weakness in Käsemann. The Apocalyptists focused so much upon the end of history that they did not understand the significant place of Christ in history, i.e. His life, teaching, death, and resurrection. Those who fail to comprehend this point forsake the central truth of Pauline eschatology.

Though the Similitudes and the Assumption of Moses contain certain Old Testament themes, we realize that each author's own vision and hope is limited by his own personal perspective. For this reason these apocalyptists do not present an organic view of the future kingdom. This is true of the books Apocalypse of Baruch (II Baruch) and 4 Esdras (4 Ezra) as well, in which the eschatological vision is a synthesis of a temporary earthly and national messianic kingdom which will be followed by the transition to a transcendent eternal kingdom in heaven.[72] This future

---

[69]J. Gresham Machen, op. cit., pp. 194-199, brings this out in respect to Paul's view of Christ. In light of the critical views in his day (which would develop into Käsemann's position), Machen believed "the apocalyptic Messiah is different in important respects from the Christ of the Epistles." He expands upon three: 1) "there is in the apocalypses no doctrine of an activity of the Messiah in creation like that which appears in I Cor. 8:6; Col. 1:16; 2) there is in the apocalypses no trace of the warm, personal relation which exists between the believer and the Pauline Christ; and 3) there is in the apocalypses no doctrine of the divinity of the Messiah."

[70]Morris, op. cit., pp. 9-12.

[71]Wayne G. Rollins, "The New Testament and Apocalyptic," New Testament Studies XVII (1970-1971), pp. 454-476.

[72]For an expanded view of the content of these books cf. Russell, op. cit., pp. 293-297. Arthur J. Ferch in his article

kingdom, also referred to as the new aeon, commences after the resurrection and judgment day.[73]

We have now examined the inconsistent eschatological view of the kingdom concept presented by the Apocalyptists. Within this inconsistent framework a pattern exists which is of interest to us: the pattern of living in this age and living for the hope of a future kingdom age (whether in heaven or on the earth or in a combination of the two), i.e. a two-age construction. "This age" (Hebrew: ha olam haz-zeh; Greek: ho aiōn hautos) is characteristically evil and is dominated by the powers of evil, whereas the future kingdom age, or more specifically, the "age to come" (Hebrew: ha olam hab-ba'; Greek: ho aiōn mellōn) is characteristically a righteous kingdom in which evil will not exist.[74] The hope of the Apocalyptists is that God will destroy the present evil age and will usher in an eternal future age.[75] The Apocalyptists began to convey to their audience that God will not deliver them in this present evil age; instead, the Hebrew must endure both evil and suffering in this age. He must find comfort in the fact that the wicked and the powers of evil will be destroyed at the consummation of this evil age. The consummation will occur on the day of Vengeance, when God will execute justice upon the wicked and upon the spirit

"The two Aeons and the Messiah in Pseudo-Philo; 4 Ezra, and 2 Baruch," Andrews University Seminary Studies XV (Autumn, 1977), 151, points this out: "At the time of national catastrophe with its resultant despair these writers raised the hopes of those who, recognizing their failures, had most probably or to a large degree given up hope. The readers are thus assured that the disparity between God's promises and the realities of history would not persist. Israel and Yahweh's law would go on forever."

[73]Ibid, pp. 150,151.

[74]It has recently been stated that "the terminology of the two ages does not emerge in apocalyptic until a late stage, becoming popular only in the first century A. D."; cf. Bauckham, op. cit., p. 21 (this depends on a first century A. D. dating of the Similitudes). It could be argued, however, that this conception is found before this time because it is implied in the basic framework of the eschatology of the apocalyptic. Vos believed this argument had credibility in his Pauline Eschatology, p. 16.

[75]One must keep in mind that the apocalyptic substance of two ages is no different from the substance of the kingdom. The age to come like that of the kingdom is understood in primarily political, national, and provisional terms. Any ethical reference is to be understood in an ethnic and legal context.

of evil. That day marks the end of this age and the beginning of the age to come. In this new age the Hebrew finds exaltation, salvation, righteousness, and faithfulness because corruption will have passed.

Some of the Apocalyptists believed that this present evil age was "fast coming to its end" (II Esd. 4.26). The eternal age, which was soon to dawn, would provide a marked contrast to the previous age for the Jew:
> Then the times shall perish, and there shall be no year, nor month, nor day, and there shall be no hours nor shall they be reckoned. There shall be one eternity, and all the just who shall escape the great judgment of the Lord shall be gathered together and they shall be eternal. Moreover, there shall be no labour, nor sickness, nor sorrow, nor anxiety, nor need, nor night, nor darkness, but a great light...and incorruptible paradise shall be their protection, and their eternal habitation. For all corruptible things shall vanish, and there shall be eternal life. (II Enoch 65.7-10)

Given this background, one immediately perceives within this context that one cannot fail to realize that the Apocalyptists presented a negative view of history upon the earth in this present age. Their eschatological presentation of the kingdom and the two-ages led only to a pessimistic and defeatist attitude toward history.[76] In reality "the Apocalyptists were indifferent to the real business of living in this world and indulged their fantasy in mere escapist speculation about a transcendent world to come."[77] Their hope is anchored only in the world to come, and thus, they picture God as a deterministic being "leaving man with no motive for responsible involvement in the course of history."[78] The Jew reclined, waited and hoped for the day when the age to come would free him from his historical predicament. All of this does not mean, however that the Jew living in this period lost his historical consciousness nor that he was not genuinely concerned for the world in which he presently lived. His negative view of history in this world did not eliminate these elements of

[76] cf. Morris, op. cit., pp. 37-41.
[77] Bauckham, op. cit., p. 19.
[78] Ibid. Morris, op. cit., pp. 45-47 also refers to this deterministic element.

his existence; instead, it intensified the hope for the age to come.

We have now seen that the apocalyptic literature presents a substantially inconsistent eschatological picture. With this in mind, we are now ready to discuss Paul's two-age construction. From this discussion it should be even more evident that Käsemann's viewpoint is not justified and that Paul's eschatological formulation has an organic and unique place in God's revelation.

Chapter 2

PAUL'S TWO-AGE CONSTRUCTION

As one studies the life and work of the Apostle Paul, it becomes clear that he absorbed himself in the person and work of Jesus Christ. Paul's confrontation by the actual ascended Christ on the road to Damascus brings forth startlingly and comprehensively a Messianic theology. Johannes Munck writes that scholars have been reluctant to endorse Luke's account of the confrontation on the Damascus road because they have thought "that such a complete change of course could not be effected so suddenly and without preparation, and that there must have been something in Paul's earlier life which predisposed him towards it, some previous history that could explain the meeting with Christ near Damascus. The attempted explanations are numerous, and vary greatly in value."[1] These explanations assert that Paul rooted his theology in the mystery religions, the emperor cult, Stoic philosophy, Platonic philosophy, pre-Christian Gnosticism, Jewish Hellenism, apocalyptic literature, or a religion of Seinverständnis. I do not find Paul's theology to be rooted in these misconceptions, but only in the death, resurrection and ascension of Christ.[2] It was Christ's confrontation of Paul that produced a radical and unique transformation in Paul's thinking and in his way of life.[3]

According to Paul, Christ is the mystery and the central point of the redemptive revelation of God (Gal. 1:11-17). Jesus Christ is the mystery of

---

[1] Paul and the Salvation of Mankind (London: SCM Press LTD, 1959), p.11.
[2] In close agreement with this point is Joachim Jeremias, "The Key to Pauline Theology," The Expository Times, LXXVI (1964), 28, and Herman Ridderbos, Paul and Jesus: Origin and General Character of Paul's Preaching of Christ, trans. David H. Freeman (Philadelphia: The Presbyterian and Reformed Publishing Company, 1958), pp. 64,65. It should also be remembered that Paul's conversion, in abstraction, is not the key to his theology; rather, the object of his conversion serves as the key, the resurrected and ascended Jesus Christ.
[3] As Munck, op. cit., p. 24, states: "Christ's revelation is not the final phase or the necessary result of Paul's inner development; on the contrary, the texts show Christ meeting Paul as his opponent, and forcing him into obedience to him and into the service of the Gentiles."

salvation which has now been fully revealed, and thus, Paul understands that through the coming of Christ a new historical period has dawned (Rom. 16:25,26; I Cor. 2:7; Eph. 1:9,10; 3:3-5; Col. 1:26; 2:2,3; II Tim. 1:9,10; Titus 1:2,3). This is a truth Paul has never before conceived. God has ushered in the last days of salvation in His risen Son. Thus at the center of Paul's existence is a Christology oriented toward eschatology.[4] We can say, therefore, that Paul understands the soteriological benefits of being in Christ to be organically tied to the eschatological work of Christ in time and space (Rom. 4:5; 5:1-5; 8:1-4; 8:28-30; Col. 1:15-20; 3:1-4; I Cor. 15:1-34).[5]

The viewpoint that the true meaning of the death, resurrection, and ascension of Jesus Christ is found in time and space is missing in Rudolf Bultmann's interpretation of Paul.[6] One reason for its absence is that Bultmann is committed to his Lutheran heritage, which he places within a modern existential framework. Lutheran tradition views Paul's theology anthropologically, which means that the starting point is the

[4]William Manson is basically correct when he writes in his article "Eschatology in the New Testament," Eschatology, no. 2, Scottish Journal of Theology Occasional Papers (Edinburgh: Oliver and Boyd LTD, 1953), p.2, that "Jesus is the subject of the New Testament religion. Eschatology is the predicate. The subject is not subordinated to the predicate but the predicate to the subject. Eschatology is made plastic to Jesus Christ." Though Manson correctly sees Christology as the key to New Testament eschatology, this writer does not care for the term "subordinate." I would rather opt for the term "component," i.e. eschatology is a component of Christology.

[5]Ridderbos, Paul and Jesus, p. 65, expresses the centrality of Christ in Paul's theology: "Paul's entire doctrine of redemption is, therefore, in all its aspects, a proclamation and explication of the redemption which has come in Christ as the fulfillment of salvation. Paul's eschatology is messianology, Christology." cf. also his work Paul: An Outline of His Theology, trans. John Richard deWitt (Grand Rapids: Wm. B. Eerdmans Publishing Company, 1975), p. 44.

[6]Even Bultmann himself speaks of his disagreement with this concept in his article "History of Salvation and History," Existence and Faith: Shorter Writings of Rudolf Bultmann, ed. Schubert M. Ogden (London: Hodder and Stoughton, 1960), pp. 226ff. Consult also Oscar Cullmann's criticism of Bultmann's position in Salvation in History, trans. Sidney G. Sowers (New York: Harper and Row, Publishers, 1967), pp. 45-47.

special soteriological principle of justifying faith. Bultmann leaves no doubt of his commitment to this tradition when he states:

> Therefore, Paul's theology can best be treated as his doctrine of man: first, of man prior to the revelation of faith, and second of man under faith, for in this way the anthropological and soteriological orientation of Paul's theology is brought out. Such a presentation presupposes, since theological understanding has its origin in faith, that man prior to the revelation of faith is so depicted by Paul as he is retrospectively seen from the standpoint of faith.[8]

Whether Bultmann is discussing Paul's view of history, eschatology, or Christology, we should understand that he bases his discussion on Paul's anthropology.[9] Unlike the Lutheran fathers of the Reformation, however, Bultmann's anthropological interpretation of Paul is immersed in existentialism. His idea of myth will serve to illustrate this.

In understanding the New Testament as "essentially mythical," he writes that "if the truth of the New Testament proclamation is to be preserved, the only way is to demythologize it."[10] If one is to demythologize, however, one must ascertain what a myth is as well as what it conveys. According to Bultmann, "the real purpose of myth is not to present an objective picture of the world as it is, but to express man's understanding of himself in the world in which he lives. Myth is an expression of man's conviction that the origin and purpose of the world in which he lives are to be sought not within it but beyond it, that is, beyond the realms of known and tangible reality."[11] In ascribing this conception

---

[7]This point is clearly made by Abraham Kuyper in his *Lectures on Calvinism* (Grand Rapids: Wm. B. Eerdmans Publishing Company, 1953), p. 21, presented at Princeton University in 1898.

[8]Rudolf Bultmann, *Theology of the New Testament*, trans. Kendrick Grobel, I (New York: Charles Scribner's Sons, 1951), p. 191. Günther Bornkamm, *Paul*, trans. D. M. G. Stalker (New York: Harper and Row, Publishers, 1971), pp. 118,119, also agrees with Bultmann's approach to Paul.

[9]cf. Rudolf Bultmann, *The Presence of Eternity: History and Eschatology* (New York: Harper and Brothers, 1957), pp. 40-42, and Bultmann, *Theology of the New Testament*, I, p. 191.

[10]Rudolf Bultmann, "New Testament and Mythology," *Kerygma and Myth: A Theological Debate*, ed. Hans Werner Bartsch (New York: Harper Torch Books, 1961), p. 10.

[11]Ibid., pp. 10,11.

of myth to the New Testament, Bultmann believes that "myth should be interpreted not cosmologically, but anthropologically, or better still, existentially."[12] For this reason "the importance of the New Testament mythology lies not in its imagery but in the understanding of existence which it enshrines."[13]

I agree with Neill Q. Hamilton in his observation that Bultmann's anthropological-existential interpretation of Paul forsakes the "real intention" of Paul's theology.[14] It is absurd to make Paul conform to modern existential categories. By doing so, Bultmann reduces Paul's conception of "eschatological age to come and the Spirit which is the agent of that age, to merely subjective experiences of the 'man of faith.'"[15] Bultmann never penetrated the richness of the Calvinistic tradition, which understands Paul as a person who submitted himself totally to the sovereignty of God. Calvinists view Paul's message as cosmologically Christocentric (in a non-mythical sense), which means that it is also objectively redemptive-historical. It is from this perspective that we now proceed with Paul's two-age construction.

The cosmic role of Christ in God's sovereign plan is central to Paul's writings.[16] Paul's Christocentric eschatology is determined solely by the sovereign plan of God as it is revealed historically in Jesus Christ. God interprets to Paul the process of His eschatological revelation as He affirms the fulfillment of redemption and tells of the expected consummation of that redemption in Christ. On the one hand, therefore Paul states that the new creation has been fulfilled because we have entered into the fulness of time (Gal. 4:4; II Cor. 5:17; 6:2), and on the other hand he asserts that the believer still lives in the present evil world with the expectation that it will cease (Rom. 8:18; 11:15; 12:2).[17] Ridder-

[12]Ibid.
[13]Ibid., p. 11.
[14]Neill Q. Hamilton, *The Holy Spirit and Eschatology in Paul* (Edinburgh: Oliver and Boyd LTD. 1957), p. 81.
[15]Ibid.
[16]We find Ridderbos, *Paul and Jesus*, p. 120, defending this point when he writes: "It seems irrefutable, however, that Paul does not base his Christology upon the motifs of a more or less dualistic cosmology, but rather upon the *history of salvation*, which finds its foundation in the creation of the world."
[17]Ridderbos, *Paul*, p. 52.

bos provides this brief description of the tension between fulfillment and expectation in Paul's eschatology:
> Of the new world, denoted in the Jewish usage as the world to come, he makes mention exclusively in a future sense (Eph. 1:21; cf. 2:7). And he does speak of the present world time in which the church is living as 'the last times' (I Tim. 4:1), but sometimes the expression 'in the last days' has reference to a period that has not yet been entered upon (II Tim. 3:1). Finally to mention still another example, in one place Paul can speak of 'the present evil aeon' as of a situation from which Christ has snatched his people (Gal. 1:4), and he can reproach the church for having subjected itself to all manner of commandments 'as if still living in the world' (Col. 2:21; cf. Eph. 2:2), while elsewhere he speaks of the present aeon and of the world as the place where the believers must live godly lives (Titus 2:12), and must shine as stars (Phil. 2:15). The result is that in certain contexts he qualifies the unredeemed life prior to the redemptive time as a 'once', 'in that time', etc. which has now been overcome (cf. Eph. 2:2, 12), in contrast with present 'now' of the new creation, the time of redemption and fulfillment (II Cor. 6:2; Eph. 2:3; Rom. 3:21 et. al.). Elsewhere, however, the 'at present' or 'now' indicates the continuance of the mode of existence defined by the world, over against the 'then' or 'once' of the perfection still to be expected (I Cor. 13:10, 12 et. al.).[18]

At this point we must observe that the distinctiveness of Paul's eschatology becomes clear in his ambiguous use of the word "now." In some contexts "now" has the meaning of the fulfillment of the time of salvation; in other contexts, it means that we are still enduring the struggles of the world. Following this pattern, New Testament scholars have described this ambiguity of the term "now" as the "already" and the "not yet." One may wonder whether this ambiguity beclouds Paul's teaching about eschatology. The clear answer, of course, is that it does not.

Nevertheless, many scholars have attempted to provide a sophisticated explanation of the pattern of the "already" and the "not yet." For example,

[18] Ibid.

some scholars have attempted to analyze Paul's eschatological formulation of the "already" and the "not yet" in terms of a traditional Jewish apocalyptic eschatological scheme.[19] Others have analyzed Paul as a thinker who systematized the aeons. But all such analyses fail. As we have seen in the previous chapter, Jewish apocalyptic literature presents its readers with an inconsistent view of eschatology. If one were to assert that this inconsistent viewpoint is the "fundamental schema" in Paul's eschatological formulation, then one would have to come to "highly dubious and untenable exegeses of certain Pauline pronouncements" (e.g. those passages that speak of the redemption and exaltation of gentiles as well as Jews).[20] I believe, therefore, that the position which states that Paul's eschatological formulation was dependent upon the apocalypists is untenable.

It also seems to me that it is unfair to make Paul's formulation of the "already" and the "not yet" fit into a rational scheme of aeons dictated by man's principles of logic. Nowhere in Paul's writings do we find a systematic eschatological timetable presented to the church. We merely see a "mingling of two ages" in which the death, resurrection, and ascension of Christ are viewed as the "breaking through of the future aeon into the present aeon." Paul views the future as present. Paul was not, therefore a "theologian who thought in terms of the aeons" just to systematize his eschatology.[21] Rather, Paul was a preacher of Jesus Christ, who has come and is yet

___

[19]cf. Klaus Koch, The Rediscovery of Apocalyptic (London: SCM Press LTD, 1972), pp. 69,70.

[20]Ibid., p. 53. For an example, we believe it is fair to make this point apply directly to Rudolf Bultmann. The reason Bultmann's understanding of the primitive Christian community and Paul are highly dubious and untenable is because Bultmann makes traditional Jewish apocalypticism the controlling factor of Paul's eschatology instead of Christ. In his article, "Man Between the Times According to the New Testament," Existence and Faith, selected and trans. Schubert M. Ogden (London: Hodder and Stoughton, 1960), p. 248, Bultmann writes, "the primitive community [Christian] interprets its present according to the scheme of traditional Jewish apocalypticism, i.e. the scheme of mythological eschatology, and its doctrine of the two aeons." Emil Brunner, Eternal Hope, trans. Harold Knight (London: Lutterworth Press, 1954), pp. 114-116, agrees with Bultmann's position.

[21]This viewpoint is found in the work by Hans Joachim Shoeps entitled Paul: The Theology of the Apostle in the Light of Jewish Religious History trans. Harold Knight (Philadelphia: The Westminster Press, 1961). John G. Gager, in his article "Func-

to come. The two aeons fit within the complete revelation of Christ in history.

Although ambiguity accompanies Paul's use of the term "now," nevertheless, when we focus our attention upon the complete revelation of Christ, Paul's formulation has a unique and clear message. It is unique and clear simply because he preaches Jesus Christ, who has come and is yet to come.[22] It does not concern Paul, however, that he uses certain eschatological terminology in reference to the present and in other places uses the same terminology with reference to the future. Whether speaking of the present or the future, Paul's concern is the revelation of Jesus Christ as the Messiah. Ridderbos makes this point clear:

> Who Christ is and what he does, what the relationship is between the time of salvation that has been entered upon with him and the future still to be expected, all this is not determined by eschatological-theological presuppositions, but is only gathered by the apostle from the unexpected and overwhelming manner in which God in Jesus Christ has given and will give the fulfillment of the redemptive promise.[23]

Paul's eschatology, in its clearest form, is the complete revelation of Jesus Christ brought about by the providential hand of God the Father. Christ comes "in the fulness of time" as the new creation. He is the fulfillment of the redemptive and covenantal work of God, which is yet to be consummated (Gal. 4:4; II Cor. 5:17; 6:2). Therefore, as we focus upon the two-age construction we must keep in mind that Christ is simply and thoroughly its center. It is Christ who provides the fundamental structure of his eschatological scheme.

tional Diversity in Paul's Use of End-Time Language," Journal of Biblical Literature, LXXXIX (1970), 325-337, points out that Paul's eschatology is unsystematic. Gager's article focuses upon the function of Paul's eschatology rather than the content or meaning of it.

[22]This is defended by Ridderbos, Paul, p. 53.

[23]Ridderbos, Paul, p. 53. Vos, Pauline Eschatology, p. 28, provides further enlightenment here: "For to Paul the chief actor in this drama had come upon the scene; the Messiah had been made present, and could not but be looked upon as henceforth the dominating figure in all further developments. And Christ was to Paul so close, so all-comprehensive and all-pervasive, that nothing could remain peripheral wherein He occupied the central place."

Christ's death and resurrection have ushered in a new historical aeon; a new aeon has begun in contrast to an old aeon. This new aeon reveals all the benefits of redemption to the believer in Christ. The believer is a member of the new aeon and participates in those benefits. The believer has died to the unredeemed world of the old aeon, i.e. the world under the curse of sin by virtue of the Fall. At the same time, he has been resurrected into the victorious life of Christ --- the new aeon (Rom. 6:6-14; Col. 3:14). The two aeons are therefore historical, whereas their contents are antithetical to each other. These aeons are fundamental to the structure of Paul's Christocentric eschatological scheme. Before we discuss any further the theological content of the two aeons, let us first discuss the words aiōn and kosmos as they are used by Paul. This will provide justification for our understanding of the two aeons which will be expressed later.

The expression "this age" (ho aiōn houtos) occurs seven times in Paul's epistles (Rom. 12:2; I Cor. 1:20; 2:6, 8; 3:18; and II Cor. 4:4). In Galatians 1:4 we find the expression "the present evil age" (ho aiōn ho enestōs ponēros), whereas in the Pastoral Epistles (I Tim. 6:17; II Tim. 4:10; Titus 2:12) we find the phrase "the present age" (ho nun aiōn). If we were to focus upon the word aeon itself, our attention would be directed toward a chronological concept. This is also true when it is connected with certain modifiers which appear in the phrases "this aeon," "this present aeon," or "this present evil aeon."[24] In Pauline theology, however, such phrases not only refer to chronological time; they also generally impart an ethical flavor.[25] In the history of redemption, therefore, "this age" is the period under the domain of Satan who is "the god of this aeon" (II Cor. 4:4). "This age" was initiated by Adam's fall into sin (Gen. 3), and it is characterized by sinfulness, unrighteousness, and the works of the flesh.[26] The principalities and powers of "this age" are

[24] Robert Law, "World," DAC, II, p. 693, brings this out when he writes, "aiōn houtos is primarily a time-concept..."

[25] Some have mentioned I Tim. 6:17 and Titus 2:12 as possible exceptions to this ethical flavor, but this could be debated.

[26] The ethical sinfulness of "this age" is summarized by Vos, Pauline Eschatology, pp. 12,13: "Such is plainly the case in I Cor. 1:20; 2:6-8; in both these instances the evil implied or expressed has a peculiar noetic reference. Satan is in II Cor. 4:4 called outright 'the god of this aeon.' According to

deliberately opposed to Christ and His believers (Rom. 8:37-39). Nevertheless, Paul teaches that even in "this age" Christ rules (Eph. 1:21).

In Ephesians 1:21 Paul mentions not only the present evil aeon but also the age to come: "Far above all rule and authority and power and dominion and every name that is named, not only in this age, but also in the one to come." Both ages appear together in this passage for the purpose of proclaiming "without restriction either as to time or sphere" the supreme, exalted name of Jesus Christ above every name.[27] One of Paul's concerns in Ephesians 1:21 is the importance of Christ in the history of redemption from its beginning (which was initiated by the fall of Adam into sin--"this age") to its consummation, when "this age" will cease and the "age to come" will stand forever.[28] Even in the midst of "this age," Paul clearly asserts that Christ already exercises His authority and power by virtue of His death, resurrection, and ascension. The exalted Christ rules in "this age" as He brings "this age" to its chronological termination and as He destroys its evil ethical milieu.

In close alliance with Paul's use of the word aeon is his use of the word kosmos. Ephesians 2:2 demonstrates this. Both terms appear in the phrase,

Gal. 1:4, Christ gave Himself for our sins that He might rescue us out of this present evil aeon. II Tim. 4:10, Demas is said to have forsaken Paul, because he loved this aeon. The Apostle warns the readers, Rom. 2:2, not to assume or bear 'the schema' of this aeon, but to let themselves be transformed in the opposite direction."

[27] Vos, Pauline Eschatology, p. 12.

[28] Edwin D. Roels, God's Mission: The Epistle to the Ephesians in Mission Perspective (Franeker: T. Wever, 1962) p. 257, realizes the broad historical reference of "this age" when he writes: "The entire period which lies between these endless ages, the time which transpires between the creation of the world and the final parousia of Christ, is commonly designated by one of a number of phrases which are translated 'this age,' 'this world,' or 'this present age.'" I commend Roels' broad historical scope of these phrases, but I cannot agree that its scope is from creation to parousia. Rather, it is from the fall to the parousia. If it is true that these phrases cannot be separated from their ethical reference, i.e. the age of unrighteousness, it therefore cannot refer to the creation, (pre-fall) which was made very good.

"wherein you once walked according to the aiōna of this kosmou." In this verse the two words are inseparable from each other though they are conceptually different from each other. In this text as well as in Rom. 3:6; I Cor. 1:20,21; 2:12; 3:14; 11:32; II Cor. 7:10; and Phil. 2:15 kosmos reflects the evil ethical notion of aeon; unlike aeon, however, the evil kosmos is seen as primarily a world and life view instead of a time view (aeon). Kosmos carries a meaning, therefore, that is closely associated with the evil connotations of the present evil aeon [as an unbeliever, one walked according to the evil age (aeon) in an evil lifestyle-kosmos].[29] Its specific reference is, however, conceptually different. Kosmos is a lifestyle or world and life view which is alienated from God and hostile to Him, manifesting the degenerate ways of sin. Therefore, the kosmos as evil is subject to the judgment of God, who will condemn and destroy it.[30] It is true that man was not evil as God created him, since God's work of creation was good. But although man was not evil as God created him, the history of redemption pictures him as a creature who became rebellious against his Creator. It is the Fall of Adam, not Adam as he was originally created by God, which initiates and necessitates this viewpoint of man. It is the notion of man as a fallen creature, that is embedded in this concept of Paul's understanding of kosmos. Kosmos is personified.

[29] Cf. Vos, Pauline Eschatology, pp. 13,24. Andrew John Bandstra, The Law and the Elements of the World: An Exegetical Study in Aspects of Paul's Teaching (Kampen: J. H. Kok N. V., 1964), p. 50, gives his consent to Vos' interpretation: "yet kosmos and aiōn may not simply be identified. While the two are interdependent, they are distinguishable entities as shown in Eph. 2:2 where it is said of men outside of Christ that they walked ton aiōna tou kosmou toutou. Rather than interpreting aeon here as a reference to a personal being, it is better to understand it as meaning that this cosmos (considered here as evil) has an end-time-or life complexia."

[30] Rudolf Bultmann, Theology of the New Testament, I, p. 255, is correct when he states that the kosmos has a connotation of a "definite theological judgment." Bultmann's statement is defended in Bandstra, op. cit., p. 49, and Geoffrey Bromiley, "World," ZPEB, V, p. 967. Bultmann writes that the "theological judgment of kosmos denotes the world of men and the sphere of human activity as being, on the one hand, a temporary thing hastening toward its end (I Cor. 7:31), and on the other hand, the sphere of antigodly power under whose sway the individual who is surrounded by it has fallen."

It has become sinful and depraved. For this reason Paul never uses the term "kosmos" in reference to the future blissful aeon, which the believer will enjoy with his Lord. Instead, he refers to a new creation in a future aeon. Bromiley is correct when he writes that "so fully is the cosmos identified with sin and the Fall that the cosmos can only be condemned and destroyed in the judgment. It comes to represent the world of evil which is in irreconcilable conflict with the world of God."[31]

Although we have seen that degenerate world and life views (kosmos) are condemned by God, nevertheless, the kosmos is still the place of God's saving work. We understand this from Paul's other meaning for the word kosmos, a meaning which signifies the inhabited world, the dwelling place of man, the scene of human history.[32] I Timothy 1:15 uses the world kosmos to mean human history: "Faithful is the saying, and it deserves full acceptance, that Christ Jesus came into the kosmon to save sinners; of whom I am foremost." Kosmos in this text can be understood as demonstrating that the world is not only the place where sinners are saved, but also that sinners are saved from this ethical evil kosmos.[33] The point here is this: just as the ethical sphere is implicit in the meaning of kosmos as a lifestyle or world and life view, likewise the ethical sphere is implicit in the meaning of kosmos as the scene of human history.

Since Paul views human history as being corrupted by sin, are we to conclude that his view of history is pessimistic? Not at all. Paul clearly teaches that God is reconciling the kosmos through Jesus Christ unto Himself (II Cor. 5:19; Rom. 11:15).[34] God's work

[31] Bromiley, op. cit.
[32] For a defense of this use of the word "kosmos" cf. Vos, Pauline Eschatology, p. 14; Bromiley, op. cit., p. 966; Law, op. cit., p. 694; George Eldon Ladd, A Theology of the New Testament (Grand Rapids: Wm. B. Eerdmans Publishing Company, 1974), p. 397; and Herman Sasse, "Kosmeō, Kosmos, Kosmios," TDNT, III, p. 888. For other uses of kosmos by Paul, cf. Ladd, op. cit., pp. 397-399; Law, op. cit., p. 694; and Sasse, op. cit., pp. 883-895.
[33] Bromiley, op. cit., p. 967
[34] I should note here that no matter how much one finds or attempts to find the thought or terminology of Hellenistic cosmology in Paul, he did not replace or denature the redemptive-historical element of his own preaching with the cosmological secular element. For Paul the cosmic effect of Christ's redemp-

continually moves toward its eschatological end: full redemption and reconciliation for His people. According to Paul, the people of God who have been reconciled in the kosmos are nothing less than members of the Kingdom of God, the future aeon, and the new creation. "Though the cosmos is the sphere and object of God's gracious work, it is still true that there is no cosmos to come,"[35] because "when the cosmos is redeemed, it ceases to be the cosmos."[36] When the believer is redeemed in Christ, therefore, he is placed in a new relationship to the world even though he has been redeemed in the world. This is evident in the way Paul speaks of the believer's identity with Christ's crucifixion. In Christ's crucifixion the world has been crucified to the believer and the believer to the world (Gal. 6:4). It is solely through Jesus Christ that the believer belongs to a new order of creation (Gal. 6:15; II Cor. 5:17); in fact, the believer has already passed through the final eschatological judgment (Gal. 3:13) and is free to live without bondage to the kosmos. The old order of things has passed away.[37] The believer is free to walk in the "wisdom" and "spirit" from above, not the "wisdom" and "spirit" of this world (I Cor. 1-3). As far as Paul is concerned, Jesus Christ came into this evil kosmos to redeem His people from this world and from its world and life views, since they are both passing away. Why? Because He wished to reveal His sovereign grace and love. He reconciled Himself with sinful man

tive work is a direct consequence of his redemptive historical preaching. Ridderbos expresses this point clearly in Paul and Jesus, pp. 120-128.

[35] Bromiley, op. cit., p. 967.

[36] Sasse, op. cit., p. 893.

[37] Writing about II Cor. 5:17, Ridderbos, Paul, p. 45 comments: "When he [Paul] speaks here of 'new creation,' this is not meant merely in an individual sense ('a new creature'), but one is to think of the new world of the re-creation that God has made to dawn in Christ, and in which everyone who is in Christ is included. This is also evident from the neuter plural that follows: 'the old things have passed away, the new have come,' and from the full significance that must be ascribed here to 'old' and 'new.' It is a matter of two worlds, not only in a spiritual, but in a redemptive-historical, eschatological sense. The 'old things' stand for the unredeemed world in its distress and sin, the 'new things' for the time of salvation and the re-creation that have dawned with Christ's resurrection. He who is in Christ, therefore, is new creation: he participates in, belongs to, this new world of God."

in order to place the people whom He had redeemed in a new kingdom, a new creation.

At this point allow me to enter into a further discussion of Paul's use of the phrase "age to come." I noted earlier that in Ephesians 1:21 Paul uses the phrase "age to come" in reference to a distinct future age. The same observation can be made concerning Ephesians 2:7, which is the only other appearance of that phrase in Paul's writings: "in order that in the ages to come he might show the exceeding riches of his grace in kindness toward us in Christ Jesus." Since each reference to the "age to come" signifies a distinct future age, Edwin D. Roels has drawn the conclusion that students of Paul must not refer to the "age to come" as already being present.[38] According to Roels, any such reference would be non-Pauline. Roels believes, therefore, that Paul adopts the Jewish conception of time as it is found in the Old Testament and in the apocalyptic literature. On the basis of this conception, the present age and the coming age would be divided by the second coming of Christ, not the first coming.[39]

As far as Roels is concerned, Christ's first coming has no distinct relevance as far as the "new age" is concerned. For example, Roels believes that the period between the death and resurrection of Christ and His second coming is to be understood as the "last days" or "this present age."[40] This, he says, is the

---

[38] Roels, op. cit., p. 259. Roels continues (p. 260) to summarize his understanding of the two-age construction: "The whole world period lying between two endless eternities and extending from the creation of the world to the second coming of Christ is designated as this age. This age, though presently evil and dominated by powers of darkness who are opposed to Christ and the believer, will be terminated by the coming of Christ, who will destroy the rulers of this age and will inaugurate the new period designated as the coming age."

[39] Ibid. This point certainly could be debated at length when one does a thorough investigation of both Old Testament and apocalyptic eschatology.

[40] cf. Roels, op. cit., p. 264. An illustration of Roels' view of redemptive history is as follows:

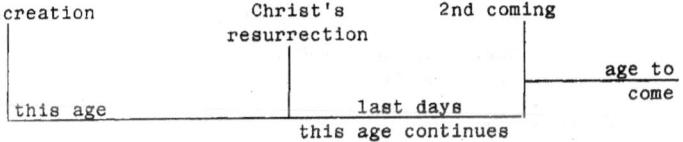

only distinctive time element that Christ's initial coming brings. Roels' conception of the "last days" has no immediate time reference to the new age. His construction denies the cosmic and historical significance of Christ's redeeming work in His first coming. This should become evident as we proceed.

It should be clear from their contexts that the two Pauline uses of the phrase the "age to come" have a distinct future reference. Although this is a true analysis of Paul's specific use of the phrase "age to come," nevertheless, many scholars have introduced the idea that the "age to come" already exists side by side with the present evil age. In other words, these scholars maintain that there is a present overlapping of the two-ages. This overlapping of the two ages must be established, however on a foundation different from the specific use of the phrase "age to come." This foundation is clearly provided by the fundamental structures of Paul's theology: the fulness of time, the revelation of the mystery, the first and last Adam, the old and new Man, flesh and spirit, Christ who is the Son of God and the Image of God, the Firstborn of every creature, and Christ the exalted and coming Kyrios.[41] These structures must also be examined in understanding Paul's two-age construction. Roels does not overlook them. He states that they "center in the crucial fact that the Messiah promised in the Old Testament, the Saviour of the world, the hope of mankind, has indeed already come, and has already granted victory and life to those who believe in him."[42] The problem with Roels' position is that he fails to acknowledge the fact that in the process of the history of redemption Christ's first coming inaugurates the new age.[43] Christ's resurrection ushers in the new age, and all the benefits of the new age have their source in Him, having been released to the believing world through His Spirit on the day of Pentecost. In my estimation, Roels has interpreted the initial coming of Jesus Christ as merely a subjective and personal application of His redemption. He has failed to acknowledge the rich historical dimension of what Christ has already accomplished in His redemptive work.

When Paul came face to face with Jesus Christ

[41] cf. Ridderbos, *Paul*, pp. 44-90.
[42] Roels, op. cit., p. 260.
[43] Bandstra, op. cit., p. 77n., criticizes Roels' view of the non-over-lapping of the ages: "It would seem that this conclu-

on the road to Damascus, he was confronted by the Creator of the new aeon of history who immediately became the center of Paul's entire existence (Col. 3:4). Paul came in contact with the one who brought the fulness of time; he actually saw the risen Lord, who is the firstfruits of them who sleep (I Cor. 15:20); he saw the Last Adam, who then made him a new man (I Cor. 15:22); he experienced the life-giving Spirit of God, who freed him from the ways of the flesh (Gal. 5:16-24); and he saw the glory of God revealed in the face of the incarnate Son of God (II Cor. 4:6). Paul saw and experienced in an intimate manner the fulness of the eternal world. The final eternal bliss of salvation became a present reality; a crucified Galilean Jew was actually the exalted ascended Son of God.

Paul tells us in II Corinthians 6:2 that Jesus Christ, therefore, is the fulfillment of redemptive time in an absolute and final sense: "Behold, now is the acceptable time; now is the day of salvation!" The phrases "the acceptable time" and "the day of salvation" correspond to the phrase "in the fulness of time" and mean "that the decisive, long-expected coming of God has dawned, the hour of hours, the day of salvation in the fulfilling, eschatological sense of the word."[44] According to Paul, the final eschatological movement toward a new creation, promised since the fall, has now come in Jesus Christ (II Cor. 5:17). Every theological idea or concept which Paul presents is shaped by the eschatological fulfillment of Christ, and thus, this fulfillment becomes the norm of Paul's entire existence. This becomes evident as we look at a few pertinent examples of Paul's ideas or concepts, keeping in mind that we are demonstrating the present overlapping of the two ages.

Paul's use of the words firstborn, firstfruits, and the beginning must be understood in a redemptive-eschatological sense. Colossians 1:15 and 18 tells us that Christ is "the firstborn of all creation" and also "the beginning, the firstborn from the dead, that in all things he might have the preeminence."

sion does not allow sufficiently for the fact that the coming age, while still future as far as the historical process is concerned, is nevertheless <u>already</u> now <u>realized</u> <u>in</u> <u>Christ</u>. This fact would best explain why Paul speaks of the Christian citizenship, life, and blessings of salvation as being 'above' or 'in heaven', etc."

[44] Ridderbos, Paul, p. 45.

Paul uses the term "firstborn" in the same way the Old Testament uses it (Ex. 4:22; Ps. 89:27): to denote "uniqueness, special status and dignity, making one as the recipient of exceptional favor and blessings."[45] Christ has this special status and place of dignity in the eternal plan of His Father because of his activity in creation and because of His exaltation over the creation.

But Christ also has this unique position because he is in union with His people. This is demonstrated by the fact that he is the "firstborn from the dead." In other words, "only as he is part of that group which is (to be) raised does he enjoy this exalted status."[46] The term, "the beginning," which precedes "firstborn," also has this meaning; the two terms go together. We should note, however, that our English word "beginning" is not a good translation of Paul's use of <u>archē</u> in this context.[47] The point is not merely that Christ is first or the beginning in the sense of chronological priority, but that He is "the Pioneer, the Inaugurator, who opened up the way" of the resurrection of His people.[48] Christ as the "firstborn" and the "beginning" has ushered in a new world, a world of resurrection, incorruptible and immortal (II Tim. 1:10; cf. also Rom. 8:29). Paul even speaks of this idea as already being present in the experience of the believer; the believer already participates in this resurrection world by faith in Christ, who is the beginning, the firstborn.[49] The believer is united with Christ through Christ's resurrection. This means that the "age to come" has begun (notice the past tense of <u>sunēgerthēte</u> in Col. 3:1). It is the "age of the resurrection life" in contrast to an age which exists for the "elements of this world"

---

[45]Richard B. Gaffin, Jr., <u>The Centrality of the Resurrection: A Study in Paul's Soteriology</u> (Grand Rapids: Baker Book House, 1978), p. 37. cf. also Ridderbos, <u>Paul</u>, p. 56. cf. Wilhelm Michaelis, "prototokos," <u>TDNT</u>, VI, p. 877.

[46]Gaffin, op. cit., p. 38.

[47]Ridderbos, <u>Paul</u>, p. 56.

[48]Ibid.

[49]It is interesting that in the book of Colossians, Paul further clarifies this point of resurrection-union in 3:1-4. He emphasizes that the believer, through Christ's resurrection, already has the resurrection as his own possession. It is because he has this as possession that he is to live a godly life: "If then you were raised together with Christ, seek the things above, where Christ is..."

(Col. 2:20; cf. also Col 3:1-17).

Paul also understands Christ as the "firstfruits" of those who are asleep (I Cor. 15:20ff). The concept that Christ is the "firstfruits" is similar to the concepts of Christ as "firstborn" and the "beginning." The term "firstfruits" is rooted also in the Old Testament.[50] As applied to the Old Testament sacrifices and offerings, the "firstfruits" idea expresses "the notion of organic connection and unity, the inseparability of the initial quantity from the whole."[51] The firstfruit represented the total harvest. Paul applies this term to the coming of Christ in the fulness of time. He is the "firstfruits" of the resurrection harvest of His people. In other words, Christ's resurrection is the beginning of the resurrection of the believers. The two resurrections are unified and inseparable. As Gaffin points out, "Paul views the two resurrections not so much as two events but as two episodes of the same event. At the same time, however, he clearly maintains a temporal distinction between them" (cf. v. 23).[52] Christ, in union with believers, represents the commencement of the new world of God.[53]

Paul's formulation of the first and last Adam appears in the context of his discussion of the "firstfruits" (I Cor. 15:21-22; cf. also I Cor. 15:42-49). The former appears because of its continuity with the latter: the two Adams concept strengthens Paul's presentation of Christ as "the firstfruits of those who are asleep." This is clear from the epeidē gar (for since) which appears at the beginning of verse 21 and reflects upon verse 20. In other words, we can say that Christ is "the firstfruits of those who are asleep" because He is the living risen Adam as opposed to the first Adam who brought death (vs. 21, 22).

It becomes obvious that in the writings of Paul the two Adams are not only individuals but they are also representatives of two antithetical orders of life, two aeons and two historical world periods (cf. also Rom. 5:12-21). Redemptive history fits entirely within the scope of their representation. Paul under-

[50] cf. Ex. 23:19; Lev. 23:10; Nub. 15:20f; 18:8, 11f, 30; Deut. 18:4; 26:1f, 10.
[51] Gaffin, op. cit., p. 34.
[52] Ibid., p. 35.
[53] Ridderbos, Paul, p. 56.

stands the Adam of Genesis to be the "first man" (I Cor. 15:45), because he was the first human creature (there were none before him). More concretely, Adam in Genesis is called "protos" because he was the first man to disobey his Creator, thereby beginning an aeon or world of sin and death (I Cor. 15:21, 22; Rom. 5:12, 17-19, 21). All mankind as manifested by its own disobedience, participates in and is responsible for, the curse which initially came with Adam (Rom. 5:12-21). This curse of sin and death comes to expression in the fact that all human bodies are perishable. They are sown in dishonor and in weakness (I Cor. 15:42, 43, 49). According to Paul, Adam initiates an aeon which is under the bondage of disobedience and under the judgment of God (Rom. 5:16).

The antithetical representation of the two Adams can be summarized as follows: as Adam is the representative of the first aeon, so Christ is the representative of the new aeon. Adam is first because no aeon comes before him; Christ is "second" or "last" because no aeon comes between Adam and Christ and because no aeon follows Christ. Christ is the eschatological man: He brings the antithetical eschatological aeon.[54] Christ brings, therefore, a mode of existence, a world order, an aeon of history which is absolutely victorious. Although the first Adam inaugurated an aeon of death, the second Adam inaugurated the aeon of resurrection life. Thus, the believer in Christ lives in the blessings of the "eschatological Adam;" the believer is "alive" as opposed to being "dead" (Rom. 5:16-19; I Cor. 15:21,22).

In light of the preceding examination I believe one can only conclude that Paul believes two ages presently overlap. The aeon of the first Adam (sin and death) continues, even though we have entered

[54]Vos clearly states this point in the Pauline Eschatology, p. 11: "In I Corinthians 15:45-47, the presence of this antithetical orientation as clearly seen in the correspondence of the two names of Christ, 'the eschatos Adam' and the 'deuteros Man;' the opposite to the former no less than to the latter being 'the protos Man.' 'Eschatos' here bears technical meaning; it designates not so much the Adam that belongs to the order of the 'eschata,' but pointedly the One who is the last in contrast with one other who is the first; it is antithetical no less than 'deuteros.' As background of the 'protos' there was no other, so beyond 'the eschatos' there can be none further."

the aeon of the last Adam which was inaugurated by His death and resurrection (firstfruit, firstborn, beginning). This overlapping will continue until the consummation of the Kingdom of God, Christ's second coming (I Cor. 15:20). At that time, the perishable will become imperishable and the mortal will become immortal (I Cor. 15:49-53). The aeon of the first Adam will cease when it passes into eternal condemnation, whereas the aeon of the second Adam will continue as it passes into eternal glorification and exaltation.

In Paul's writings the contrasting concepts of flesh (sarx) and spirit (pneuma) correspond to the concept of the two Adams. Therefore, the conflict between the flesh and spirit is also redemptive-historical.[55] The flesh (earthly) and the spirit (heavenly) are in conflict with each other.[56] They are in a struggle, attempting to bring forth their respective manifestations (cf. Eph. 1:14, 21; 2:7, 12; 4:4, 30; 5:6; Col. 3:4; 6:24; Phil. 1:6; 2:16; 3:20). This is why Vos insists that the Hellenistic conception of the pneuma, whether in its Platonic, neo-Platonic, or Stoic form, is not Pauline; the Greek philosophical conception results in a "dualistic bisection of nature"[57] since it is not a product of the direct revelation of God. According to Paul's theology, this historical element is the controlling factor of both sarx and pneuma.[58] The sarx is evil because it has historically

---

[55] In most cases, Paul's use of the terms earthly and heavenly is synonymous to flesh and spirit.

[56] Contrary to modern critical scholarship we must remain consistent to the structure of Paul's thought, and therefore insist that his cosmology fits with and flows from this redemptive-historical scheme. As Ridderbos states: "No matter to what extent Paul may have been influenced by the thought or terminology of Hellenism, and may have placed himself in the thought world of his readers, it is certain that he did not replace or denature the redemptive historical element by the cosmological element" (Paul and Jesus, p. 120; cf. also pp. 121, 122).

[57] Vos, "The Eschatological Conception of the Spirit," p. 245.

[58] Ridderbos, When the Time Had Fully Come, p. 52, makes this quite clear: "That is why Spirit is opposed to 'flesh.' For in Paul flesh, too, is not primarily an existential notion, but a redemptive-historical one. Flesh is the mode of existence of man and the world before the fullness of the times appeared. Flesh is man and world in the powers of darkness. And opposing this is the Spirit, the Pneuma, not first and foremost as an individual experience, not even in the first place as an individual reversal, but as a new way of existence which became present time with the coming of Christ (Rom. 8:9)." In Paul, p. 205,

become evil through the entrance of sin, not because of its natural constitution. It is a mode of existence in which man and the world are under the powers of darkness. The pneuma world is a world of consummation because Jesus Christ, the long-expected Messiah, has come and has brought the final eschatological design of God. It is a mode of existence which began with the coming of Christ (Rom. 8:9). As one can see, Paul is not presenting a dualistic interpretation of nature; rather, he is presenting a simple interpretation of redemptive history.

The death, resurrection, and ascension of Jesus Christ as well as the coming of the Holy Spirit on the day of Pentecost places the believer in the eschatological aeon of the Spirit of God. In this eschatological aeon the work of the Holy Spirit is to apply the saving benefits (grace and obedience) of being in Christ to His people, His church. The work of the Holy Spirit is Christocentric, establishing and making the believer to be Christ-like, i.e. enabling the believer to walk in the Spirit of Christ (Rom. 8:2,10,11; Gal. 5:22-26).[59] The Spirit places the believer in a new creation, a new order of things. In opposition to the way of the Spirit (Gal. 5:17), the way of the flesh is governed by "the prince of sin" (Satan), who is actively working evil in the sons of disobedience (Eph. 2:2; Gal. 5:19-21). The way of the flesh

Ridderbos also writes: "The Spirit as the Spirit of Christ is the spirit of the new aeon, and all that he renews, recreated, changes, is new and different because it pertains to this eschatological 'newness'...yet it holds here as well, and perhaps to a still greater degree than in the doctrine of sin, that the great Vorverständnis of all Paul's preaching is not of an anthropological but of a redemptive-historical, eschatological, i.e. to say of a Christological and pneumatological nature." Bultmann, New Testament Theology, I, pp. 232-246, 330-340, holds to the existential concept.

[59] Neill Q. Hamilton, The Holy Spirit and Eschatology in Paul, pp. 3,9, parallel to Vos, writes concerning the relationship between Christ and the Spirit, "Thus the common opinion is correct which sees the key to the doctrine of the Spirit in the doctrine of Christ...For the moment it suffices to note the Christocentric foundation for action of the Spirit which Paul here lays. The Spirit not only transmits the benefits of Christ and so makes Christ present to faith, but also promotes that recognition of the Lordship of Jesus which is the birth of faith." It is at this point that Hamilton is very critical of Bultmann. He writes: "He [Bultmann] does not find it necessary to emphasize the Christological aspect of the Spirit. This is probably

corresponds to the present evil aeon and its order of things-the old creation in its distance from God.[60] The believer has been redeemed from this evil world, and is therefore ruled by the eschatological Spirit of God.[61] The fact remains, however, that the believer is still in the world of the flesh. The believer is engaged, therefore, in an eschatological tension: he lives in the eternal world of the Spirit of God, but the temporal world of the flesh surrounds him. This eschatological tension can be examined in two ways: 1) in its temporal situation, that of being in the world but not of the world, and 2) in the conflict of the "already-not yet." Let us begin with the former.

The key to the believer's existence within this tension is a Christocentric soteriology. The believer has been crucified to the temporal world: his sins of the flesh are dead (Rom. 6:6, 7, 9, 11; Col. 3:3; Gal. 6:15). He is now living, therefore, in the victory of Christ's resurrection as a person who by faith is already experiencing a resurrection union with Christ (Rom. 6:5, 9, 10; Col. 3:1-4). By faith, the believer has entered into the sphere of the heavenly, and now sits in the heavenly places with his Savior who has all authority and dominion (Eph. 1:20, 21; 2:6). The believer enjoys his present citizenship in heaven

so for two reasons. First, the ministry, death and resurrection of Christ are not the kind of events that could in any forensic or historical way provide a basis for the Spirit's release and activity among believers. And second, it is understandable that he should not press the implications of Christology or eschatology for the doctrine of the Spirit, for in the back of his mind the Spirit is something that has no ultimate reality" (p. 82).

[60]This point concerning *sarx* is stated by John A. T. Robinson, The Body: A Study in Pauline Theology (London: SCM Press LTD, 1952), p. 31.

[61]It is definitely true that the work of the Holy Spirit in the believer is eschatologically and redemptive-historically qualified. Ridderbos, When the Time Had Fully Come, p. 52 puts it like this: "This being in the Spirit is not mystical, but is an eschatological, redemptive-historical category. It means: You are no longer in the power of the old aeon; you have passed into the new one, you are under a different authority. This is the indicative of redemption, the proclamation of the new state of life, and it can be followed by the imperative: If we live by the Spirit, let us also walk by the Spirit." That mystical conception which Ridderbos refers to was found in Albert Schweitzer's work The Mysticism of Paul the Apostle (London: A. & C. Black, 1953), pp. 13, 160-166.

(Phil. 3:19, 20), and as a citizen of heaven, he is commanded to seek and to set his mind upon the things that are in heaven, not upon things of the fleshly world (Col. 3:2).[62] Here lies the eschatological tension for the believer: although the believer is already in heaven and he is commanded to seek and set his mind on the things that are above, he nevertheless finds himself suffering through the torments of the present evil world (I Cor. 4:11, 13; Rom. 8:18ff). He is in a constant battle with the flesh and with the powers of evil (Gal. 5:16ff; Eph. 6:12). In fact, Paul's pastoral concern is that his readers understand that "this world" is still an evil place of temptation and trial. Nevertheless, the believer must be transformed by renewing his mind in Jesus Christ; doing so, he will not be conformed to "this age" (Rom. 12: 1, 2).

A point of controversy arises here. Are believers to be understood as citizens of two worlds (aeons) while they live upon the earth? Ragnar Leivestad takes the position that Paul understands the believer to be a citizen of both aeons. He writes:

> There is a certain obsurity concerning the victory over the powers due to the transitional state in which the apostle is living. The old age is passing away, and the new is coming. The new age has begun, while the old has not yet vanished. Those living between the resurrection of Jesus and his *parousia* belong to two ages at the same time; they are citizens of two worlds. In Christ they are new creatures belonging to the age of resurrection, but as long as they are still in the body they are subject to the conditions of this world. If the cosmic rulers have in principle been dethroned at the resurrection of Christ, they continue to exercise authority as long as the old cosmos has not been succeeded by the new. If in principle we have already died to sin and the law, we have yet to fight against temptations coming through the flesh.[63]

---

[62] As Vincent Taylor tells us in *Forgiveness and Reconciliation: A Study in New Testament Theology* (London: Macmillan and Company, Limited, 1941), p. 140: "For our [believer's] citizenship is in heaven; the believer lives on earth, but already here and now his true life is that of the Age to come."

[63] Ragnar Leivestad, *Christ the Conqueror: Ideas of Conflict and Victory in the New Testament* (London: SPCK, 1954), p. 96. In his article entitled "New Testament Eschatology," *Scottish*

Although we can sympathize with the problem of obscurity to which Leivestad refers, I nevertheless fail to see why we should conclude that Paul regards the believer as a citizen of two worlds. In my estimation this is not what Paul is telling us. Although Paul understands that the believer is truly living in two opposing worlds (the overlapping of two aeons), he is not a citizen of the "present evil age." Paul never views the believer as separated from Christ, and therefore he never views the believer as a citizen of the world of the flesh. This Pauline concept agrees thoroughly with Christ's teaching of being *in* the "present evil aeon" (*in* the world), but being not of the "present evil aeon" (*of* the world). On the contrary, the believer is *of* the "aeon to come." His sole citizenship resides with Christ in heaven because he has been bought with the price of Christ's blood, and has therefore become Christ's possession (Phil. 3:20; I Cor. 6:19,20). After the believer has been brought into union with Christ, he is never said to be the possession of Satan or under the dominion of the ways of Satan (part of the present evil aeon).[64] Even when we deal with the controversial seventh chapter of Romans, regardless of what approach or conclusion we take to the chapter, we cannot deny that Paul is moving throughout it to the climatic doxology in praise of Christ (Rom. 7:24,25; 8:1,2). The

Journal of Theology VI (1953), 149, C. K. Barrett also holds this position, speaking of it as a "Christian paradox."

[64] David Ewert, The Spirit and the Age to Come, (Montreal: Unpublished Ph.D. Thesis at McGill University, 1969), p. 28, defends this position when he states that "nowhere do we gain the impression that a believer vacillates between two ages, never quite sure to which he belongs. We must not let the dynamic character if the new age which has moved into the present rob it of its temporal meaning." Ewert's conclusion is clear: the believer is a citizen only of the "aeon to come", the "age of the Spirit." When Paul addresses the Thessalonian church concerning the "lawless one" (II Thess. 2), his goal is not to frighten his readers; rather, it is to strengthen their confidence that they are in Christ and are therefore not in danger of this coming "lawless one" (vs. 13, 14). God sends the "lawless one" so that those who are perishing (those who are not saved) "might believe what is false" and so be judged by that wickedness (vs. 10-12). The believer needs only to remain stedfast in the gospel (vs. 15) in order to be impregnable. Even in relationship to the "lawless one," Paul continues to define the believer's existence as total union with Christ -- he is solely of the "age to come."

pinnacle of the doxology is chapter 8, verse 1: "There is therefore now no condemnation for those who are in Christ Jesus." This describes the present actual state of the believer's existence. His existence is totally immersed in the accomplished work of Christ. He is forever free from condemnation. Thus the problem of "obscurity" is resolved. Paul and fellow believers are not citizens of two aeons, but of one (the aeon to come). They struggle against the other aeon (the present evil aeon), patiently waiting for the consummating hand of God, which will destroy the present evil aeon.

In the second place, many scholars have discussed this tension in the context of the "already-not yet." I have in mind more specifically Oscar Cullmann's formulation of this idea:

> The new element in the New Testament is not eschatology, but what I call the tension between the decisive "already fulfilled" and the "not yet completed," between present and future (called "taseology" from the Greek word meaning "tension"). The whole theology of the New Testament, including Jesus' preaching, is qualified by this tension...this can have no other meaning than that salvation history is the common basis of the whole New Testament. We hold that there is in the New Testament a temporal tension between faith in a decision already made and hope resting upon it for what is not yet fulfilled.[65]

According to Cullmann, New Testament taseology is

---

[65]Oscar Cullmann, Salvation in History (London: SCM Press LTD, 1967), p. 172. cf. also Oscar Cullmann, Christ and Time: The Primitive Christian Conception of Time and History, trans. Floyd V. Filson (Philadelphia: The Westminster Press, 1975), pp. 81-93. Floyd V. Filson has also written concerning his own admiration and agreement with Cullmann's position in his work, The New Testament Against Its Environment: The Gospel of Christ the Risen Lord (London: SCM Press LTD, 1950), pp. 67,68. C. K. Barrett, From First Adam to Last: A Study in Pauline Theology (London: Adam and Charles Black, 1962), p. 105, also expresses admiration for Cullmann's position. I should mention that there are other intepretations of the eschatological tension in Paul's theology, such as Dodd's, Niebuhr's, and MacLeod's. For an explanation of their viewpoints see T. F. Torrance's article "The Modern Eschatological Debate," The Evangelical Quarterly XXV (1953), 45-54; 94-106; 167-178; 224-232. I address myself to Cullmann because he is a respected scholar and because his position is somewhat akin to that of evangelical scholars such as Vos, Ridderbos, and Gaffin.

a dialectic; it is a dialectic of the present and future, or of the already fulfilled and the not yet fulfilled.[66]

Although we are grateful to Cullmann's insight, nevertheless, I must ask whether the dialectic applies merely to the present and the future eschatological setting as he maintains.[67] It is true that Paul teaches that the believer lives within the tension of what he has already received in Christ and what he will fully receive at the <u>parousia</u> of Christ, or to put it another way, what he has not yet received. But this tension exists because the believer, living in the state of the "already," must still exist in the "present evil age"--although, as we have already noted, he is not a citizen of the "present evil age." The tension presently exists because God permits evil to continue until He finally destroys it at His Son's second coming. It is this continuation of evil and its final destruction as well as the present existence of two antithetical world orders that conditions the "already and the not yet."

The second issue that can be raised concerning Cullmann's formulation of the "already-not yet" is how should his dialectical formulation be understood? In my estimation Cullmann does not clearly define how he is using the term "dialectic." In light of this failure, he does not clearly distinguish his formulation from a critical existential interpretation of redemptive history. What is the dialectic of present and future? Is it a tension coming to expression existentially in the believer's individual existence as he acknowledges the continual kingship of Christ in redemptive history? It seems to me that this is a credible explanation of Cullmann's dialectic since he does not want to speak of a dialectic of two existing world orders, i.e. world orders which are concretely historical. Although I believe he is somewhat successful in distinguishing himself from the existential formulations of Kierkegaard and Bultmann,[68] he nevertheless fails to completely separate himself from an existential interpretation of the relationship between Christ and the believer in redemptive history.

In summary, the way of the Spirit and the way

---
[66] Cullmann, <u>Christ and Time</u>, p. 146.
[67] Ibid.
[68] cf. Ibid. and Cullmann, <u>Salvation in History</u>, pp. 45-47.

of the flesh are antithetical to each other; they represent two opposing aeons. The way of the Spirit is the eschatological aeon, the "age to come." The Holy Spirit applies to the believer all the saving benefits of Christ to the believer which are characteristic of that aeon beginning with the death, resurrection, and ascension of Christ and the coming of the Spirit on Pentecost. On the other hand, the way of the flesh is the way of evil in its distance from the being of God. In the history of redemption it is the "present evil age" which will continue until God by His providential hand extinguishes it. The message of Paul is clear. The way of the Spirit is distinctively Christian. The believer may not compromise his stand in the Spirit of God by uniting himself with the ways of the flesh. The believer must judge and understand all things from the vantage of his existence in the Spirit.

Having examined these fundamental concepts and ideas of Paul's theology (fulness of time, firstborn, firstfruits, beginning, first and last Adam, and the way of the Spirit and the way of the flesh), we clearly see two, present, overlapping aeons in Paul's redemptive-historical time-line.[69] This scheme can be drawn

---

[69]I am clearly opposed to Bultmann's existential formulation of the overlapping of the two ages. I have demanded that Paul's interpretation of redemptive history between the death, resurrection, and ascension of Jesus Christ and His parousia is that of two overlapping concrete historical periods. Bultmann affirms the overlap only in the existential decisive "now" of certain events (e.g. the kerygma) and in responses to those events (faith). The existential "now" is not the constant possession of the believer, but only occurs at a particular point along the process of time, and yet, when it occurs it is no longer an event in time. It has become an existential event. Bultmann in "A Reply to the Theses of J. Schniewind," Kerygma and Myth: A Theological Debate, ed. Hans Werner Bartsch, trans. Reginald H. Fuller (New York: Harper Torch Books, 1961), p. 114, writes: "I am surprised how readily people conclude that my interpretation of the New Testament eschatology implies a timeless 'now.' To say that two ages or cosmic periods overlap is to my mind totally inadequate. If the point of the contrast between two ages is that the present age is evil and that in the age to come there will be no more temptation or death, the age to come cannot be conceived as a further period in history or as overlapping the old age like epochs in history. The overlapping is possible and the old to come a present reality only in virtue of certain events and responses to those events within the old age. Faith interprets these as the eruption of the new age. I refer of

as follows:[70]

	The age to come realized in principle	
Resurrection of Christ	in heaven	Parousia
	on earth	Future age and world fully realized in solid existence

This present evil age or world

The diagram shows that the believer lives in two aeons during the period from the resurrection of Christ until His second coming. The believer has been horizontally exalted into the "age to come" by virtue of Christ's resurrection. There is absolutely "no escape for the Christian from its ["age to come"] supreme dominion over his life."[71] Because of this fact the Christian's whole world and life view is to be molded by the "age to come." Finally, at the parousia of Christ, the "present evil aeon" will cease and the "age to come" will reach its consummated state.

course to the event of Christ, the kerygma, the response of faith, and the Church or community of believers. What happens in these phenomena now -- i.e. at particular points along the time process -- has ceased to be an event in time. Therefore in the last analysis each particular Now is to the eyes of faith that one Now which is the fullness of time."

[70]This diagram is found in Vos, Pauline Eschatology, p. 38.
[71]Ibid.

Chapter 3

I CORINTHIANS 1-3: ANTITHETICAL WISDOM

Paul clearly teaches that the great expected day of the Lord's salvation has dawned. The new creation has already begun in the death, resurrection, and ascension of Jesus Christ and now waits for the parousia of Christ. The New Testament church is already the eschatological community. But as we saw in the previous chapter, the church exists during this period in the tension of two aeons. Paul expresses this tension in I Corinthians 1-3 in terms of the wisdom of the world over against the wisdom of God. More specifically, this tension is initially addressed to the Corinthian church (chapters 1-3) in terms of the "wisdom of the world" over against the "word of the cross."[1] The problem of strife among the members of the Corinthian congregation (1:10-16) was a symptom of the tension between the "wisdom of the world" and the "word of the cross." Because the Corinthians had failed to make a proper distinction between these two wisdoms, they were divided among themselves. In other words, this division brought to mind in the Apostle Paul the contrast of two modes of existence, two world orders. Paul impresses upon the members of the Corinthian church that the saving benefits of the "age to come" have become present through the revelation of God's redemption, Jesus Christ (1:1-9,30; 2:7,13). On the other hand, those who reject the revelation of God in His Son are members of the "present evil aeon," basing their wisdom in this world rather than the "word of the cross" (1:20; 2:6). Paul is warning the Corinthians that their response to the revelation of Christ is following the authority of men (1:12), and thus, they are acting as the world acts (3:1-3). Paul is not comfortable with this. His desire is to see them tear down their barriers of strife and become truly one in Christ (1:10),[2] through whom the church can stengthen its

---

[1] cf. Robert W. Funk, Language, Hermeneutic, and Word of God: The Problem of Language in the New Testament and Contemporary Theology (New York: Harper and Row, Publishers, 1966), p. 275. Also Günther Bornkamm, Paul, p. 159, writes: "Paul expresses his concern in I Corinthians through a sharp contrast between 'the word of the cross' and 'the wisdom of this world' (I Cor. 1:18-3:20)."

[2] Charles Hodge, An Exposition of the First Epistle to the Corinthians (Grand Rapids: Wm. B. Eerdmans Publishing Company, 1956), p. 12.

unity against the only enemy of Christ's Kingdom, the "wisdom of this world." If the enemy is going to be defeated, Christ must be present in the church. Paul obviously believes that Christ is present in the Corinthian church. This is evident by the fact that he addresses the Corinthian church in terms of its identity in Christ and its separation from the world (1:2).[3] He wants, therefore, to arouse in the conscience of every believer at Corinth the fact that they are to be living in the power and wisdom of God alone (1:24; 2:4,5), totally distinct from the ways of the world, responding to the "word of the cross" in submission to their Redeemer.

The problem that Paul faced in Corinth was, therefore, the failure of the church to understand eschatological living as it results from the redemp-

---

[3] This concept can be seen quite simply in the phrase "those [members of the Corinthian church] who have been sanctified in Christ Jesus." George Eldon Ladd, A Theology of the New Testament, pp. 519, 520, 544, writes concerning this phrase: "When applied to the Christian [sanctification], holiness or sanctification is not in the first place an ethical concept although it includes the ethical aspect. It denotes first of all a soteriological truth that Christians belong to God. They are God's people. This is why the most common use of hagios in Paul is to designate all Christians as saints, the people of God. Christians are holy even in their bodily existence when they give themselves to God (Rom. 12:1)...even more important than this is the fact that all believers are viewed as already sanctified in Christ. In this sense, sanctification does not designate growth in ethical conduct but is a redemptive truth. Paul addresses the Corinthians among whom existed scandalous sins not only as saints but as those sanctified in Christ Jesus (I Cor. 1:2, 30). Cleansing, sanctification, justification are factual events of the past. Sanctification here means inclusion in the people whom God claims as his own...Paul's challenge to his churches was that they should realize in life and conduct what was already theirs in Christ. Because they were saints of God, they were to live holy lives." Our point here is that sanctification means redemption and identity with Christ, as well as separation from the world. Many have brought this out. For example, John Calvin comments in his Commentary on the Epistles of Paul the Apostle to the Corinthians, trans. John Pringle, I (Grand Rapids: Wm. B. Eerdmans Publishing Company, 1948), p. 52: "Hence all must be sanctified in Christ who would be reckoned among the people of God. Now the term sanctification denotes separation. This takes place in us when we are regenerated by the Spirit to newness of life, that we may serve God and not the world."

tive work of being in Christ.⁴ My position is quite different from those scholars who attempt to build a case that Paul's argument is directed toward a certain faction who is mentioned in I Corinthians 1:12: "Now this I mean, that each of you saith, I am of Paul; and I of Apollos; and I of Cephas; and I of Christ." These scholars "begin by reconstructing the single point of view which was opposed to Paul's and then seek to identify this position with one of the parties mentioned in I Cor. 1:12."⁵ This opposition, they say, governs the remaining content of I Corinthians. The Tubingen School, led by F. C. Baur,⁶ began this viewpoint. Baur takes the alleged problem addressed in II Corinthians 11:22 (cf. also Gal. 1:11ff) and applies it to I Corinthians. He believes there is a severe struggle between Paul and Peter and also among their followers (so-called "Paulinists" and "Petrinists"). The problem is a Jewish-Gentile antagonism in which the Peter and Christ parties are Jewish and the Paul and Apollos parties are Gentile.⁷ Baur identifies Paul's opponents at Corinth as the Judaist "Christ party," in which Peter is included.⁸ Baur's

⁴cf. I Corinthians 1:2,18,26,30; 2:5,10; 3:16,22,23; 4:8,14, 15; 5:7; 6:11; 7:32-34; 8:6; 9:12,14; 10:6; 11:22,23; 12:3; 13:12, 13; 14:26; 15:1,2; 16:13.

⁵John Coolidge Hurd, Jr., The Origin of I Corinthians (New York: Seabury Press, 1965), p. 97.

⁶"Die Christuspartei in der korinthischen Gemeinde, der Gegensatz des petrinischen und paulinischen Christenthumus in der ältesten Kirche," Tübinger Zeitschrift für Theologie, V (1831), 61-206.

⁷Using the principles of Hegelian philosophy, Baur sees this verse (I Cor. 1:12) as providing a key to understanding primitive Christianity. Judaism is the thesis, the Gentile Christians the antithesis, and out of this dispute the unity of the catholic church arose. cf. F. W. Grosheide, Commentary on the First Epistle to the Corinthians (Grand Rapids: Wm B. Eerdmans Publishing Company, 1953), p. 36.

⁸Although Baur's presuppositions have been rejected by modern scholarship, there are those who still maintain Paul's opponent to be Judaists belonging to the Cephas party. These men are: Wilfred Lawrence Knox, St. Paul and the Church of Jerusalem (Cambridge: The University Press, 1925), pp. 311-321; Ernst Bammel, "Herkunft und Funktion der Traditionselemente in 1. Kor. 15:1-11," Theologische Zeitschrift, XI (1955), 412; Jacques Dupont, Gnosis: La Connaissance Religieuse dans les Epitres de Saint Paul (Louvain: East Neuwelaerts, 1960), p. 258; Derk William Oostendorp, Another Jesus: A Gospel of Jewish Christian Superiority in II Corinthians (Kampen: J. H. Kok, 1967); and Schoeps, Paul: The Theology of the Apostle in the Light of Jewish

position stimulated other scholars to disagree with his theory and to present Paul's opponent as one of the other parties mentioned in I Corinthians 1:12.

Some scholars believe the Apollos party is Paul's chief opposition, since both I Corinthians (3:6) and Acts (18:24-28) mention that Apollos actually visited Corinth and worked among its people. Of the parties mentioned in I Corinthians 1:12, Apollos receives the most biblical attention. In I Corinthians 1-4, his name appears six times and thus scholars have assumed that he is at the root of the problems in Corinth. According to these scholars, Apollos serves as the "thorn in the flesh" to the Corinthian church, which Paul worked so hard to establish.[9]

What is the problem? It has been traditionally stated that 1) Apollos created a schism in the church concerning the sacrament of baptism (Acts 18:25, 26) and 2) he was an eloquent man (Acts 18:24) with the ability to speak boldly (Acts 18:26), and thus, Paul has Apollos in mind when he states that he did not use superior speech or persuasive words to preach the gospel (I Cor. 2:1,4). Because of Richard A. Horsley's work, the latter position is receiving more attention in our day whereas the former position seems to have lost credibility.[10]

Horsley believes that Paul is reacting against two aspects of *sophia* in I Corinthians 1-4: "wisdom in speech as well as wisdom as the means of salvation."[11] But what is the reason for Paul's discussion of wisdom? According to Horsley, Paul was confronting a problem that had become typical in the Hellenistic Jewish tradition represented best by Philo and the Wisdom

Religious History, pp. 78-82. There are many scholars who believe that Peter himself visited Corinth and won many people to his name. For a list of those who hold this position, cf. Hurd, op. cit., p. 100, n. 5.

[9]cf. for example Ernest Evans, The Epistles of Paul the Apostle to the Corinthians (Oxford: The Clarendon Press, 1930), p. 66, and Eric L. Titus, Essentials of New Testament Study (New York: The Roland Press Company, 1958), p. 131, n.1.

[10]"Wisdom of Words and Words of Wisdom," The Catholic Biblical Quarterly, XXXIX (April, 1977), 224-239. Consult also his article "Pneumatikos vs. Psychikos Distinctions of Spiritual Status Among the Corinthians," Harvard Theological Review, LXIX (July-October, 1976), 269-288.

[11]"Wisdom of Words and Words of Wisdom," p. 224.

of Solomon. Both Philo and the Wisdom of Solomon thought that the role of wisdom could be abused. This was evident in the great orators of Alexandria who stood in the Hellenistic Jewish tradition. The eloquence of speech could be used in such a way as to persuade people of the wisdom of God as well as their salvation. Philo and the Wisdom of Soloman state, however, that this is contrary to the divine use and content of wisdom. Horsley thinks, therefore, that the abuse of wisdom is exactly what Paul is confronting in Corinth. But in order to confront this abusive use of wisdom, it is Horsley's position that Paul followed the Hellenistic Jewish tradition of the divine use and content of wisdom. Paul did this in order to confront the Corinthian error on a common platform, i.e. the Hellenistic Jewish tradition. But how did the abusive aspect of wisdom come to Corinth? In Horsley's estimation, the historical link is found in Apollos, who was an Alexandrian Jew, and thus, had direct ties to the Hellenistic Jewish tradition and the understanding of the abuse of wisdom by eloquent and persausive speech. Interestingly Horsley proceeds to attempt to guard himself in case no direct connection can be documented between Apollos and Philo in Alexandria. He points out to us that even if no direct link can be substantiated between Philo and Apollos, nevertheless, the idea of abusive wisdom in the Hellenistic Jewish tradition was known throughout the world at this time because of the "mobility of people, ideas, and religious cults in the Hellenistic-Roman world."[12] In light of this mobility, the abusive use of wisdom came to settle in Corinth. Even in spite of guarding his position, Horsley goes on to attempt to convince us that Apollos is the source of the Corinthian problem concerning <u>sophia</u>. In the final analysis, Horsley thinks this can be credibly maintained.

In our day the most commonly held theory about Paul's opposition is the Christ party. The scholars who sympathize with this position understand the Christ party to be Jewish Christian Gnostics. According to these scholars, Paul employs certain gnostic schemes, such as the dualistic view of the world as it is antithetically set forth in the flesh-spirit. Then he reinterprets them within a Christian framework. They do not mean by this that Paul's theology is rooted in the thoroughly worked out mythological Gnosticism, but they do affirm that Paul employs many of the Gnos-

[12] Ibid., p. 231.

tic's expressions and schemes in order to correct the theology of the Christ party. Walter Schmithals, a leading exponent of this view, takes the question "Is Christ divided?" as a slogan of the Christ party. According to Schmithals, the Christ party is claiming that they are "only the spiritual followers of Christ. Is Christ divided into pieces and distributed among mere apostles (as the rival claims of the parties of Paul, Apollos and Cephas imply)?"[13] Members of the Christ party view themselves as hyperspiritual enthusiasts who have no need for any human leader. Their conception of themselves is that they are free from submitting to the revelatory message of the Apostle Paul. Thus to sober the mythical Gnosticism of the Corinthian church, Paul asserts the theology of the cross.[14]

Most scholars maintain that Paul is addressing one opponent throughout I Corinthians. But the question is whether any of the parties can be confirmed as Paul's opponent. I think not. Throughout the epistle, Paul never analyzes the various opinions of these parties,[15] nor does he admit that they believed in a false doctrine.[16] With respect to Apollos, "Paul always speaks about Apollos in the same loyal and appreciative way that he is accustomed to do about

[13] Walter Schmithals, Die Gnosis in Korinth: Eine Untersuchung zu den Korinthabriefen (Göttingen: Vandenhoeck und Ruprecht, 1956), p. 166.
[14] Other important scholars who support this view are Ulrich Wilckens, Weisheit und Torheit: Eine exegetisch-religionsgeschichtliche Untersuchung zu 1. Kor. 1 und 2 (Tübingen: J.C.B. Mohr, 1959); Rudolf Bultmann, Primitive Christianity in its Contemporary Setting, trans. R. H. Fuller (New York: The World Publishing Company, 1956), pp. 162-208; Bultmann, Kerygma and Myth, pp. 19-22; Ernst Käsemann, Das Wanderude Gottesvolk (Göttingen: Vandenhoeck und Ruprecht, 1959), pp. 61ff.; Ernst Fuchs, Die Freiheit Des Glaubens, Römer 5-8 ausgelegt (München: Chr. Kaiser Verlag, 1949), pp. 18ff., and Günther Bornkamm, Das Ende des Gesetzes (München: Chr. Kaiser Verlag, 1952), pp. 83ff.
[15] cf. James Moffatt, The First Epistle of Paul to the Corinthians (London: Hodder and Stoughton Limited, 1938), p. 9.
[16] cf. F. W. Grosheide, Commentary on the First Epistle to the Corinthians, p. 37; Jean Hering, The First Epistle of Saint Paul to the Corinthians, trans. A. W. Heathcote and P. J. Allcock (London: The Epworth Press, 1962), p. 44; and the fifth chapter of Munck's Paul and the Salvation of Mankind (p. 152) entitled "The Church without Factions: Studies in I Corinthians 1-4."

his other colleagues."[17] Paul describes his work with all his colleagues, including Apollos, as complementary (I Cor. 3:6). Apollos and Paul have, therefore, a friendly relationship (I Cor. 16:12).[18] Consequently, it seems speculative to build an argument on the basis of the term sophia and on the fact that Apollos was an eloquent and bold speaker. There is no proof that because Apollos was a Jew from Alexandria he was of necessity dominated by the Hellenistic Jewish tradition, and thus was responsible for the abusive use of sophia in Corinth. Since we do not have a digest of Apollos' thought, how can we prove that he accepted the ideas popular in Alexandria?

We recall that scholars who consider the Cephas party to be Paul's oppostion build their case on II Corinthians 11:22 ("Are they Hebrews? So am I. Are they Israelites? So am I. Are they descendants of Abraham? So am I."). They apply this text to I Corinthians, but I Corinthians is silent concerning the opinion of the Cephas party and the doctrines they represented. The theory that Paul's opposition is the Cephas faction is established only upon the erroneous assumption that inferences from other New Testament writings must be applied to the Cephas party at Corinth. There is no evidence from Paul himself that this should be done.[19]

It seems that the Christ party, which is to be understood as mythological Gnosticism also breaks down because there is no indication in I Corinthians that Paul is specifically confronting their Gnosticism. After intensive research R. M. Wilson refutes this idea:
> ...there is no gnostic myth, no gnostic system, no gnostic document which can be dated so early as to suggest influence from anything like a developed gnostic movement, like the Gnosticism of the second century ... Gnosis in the broader sense is not yet Gnosticism, and to interpret New Testament texts which may reflect Gnosis

[17] Munck, op. cit., p. 144.
[18] Leon Morris brings this out forcefully in The First Epistle of Paul to the Corinthians: An Introduction and Commentary (Grand Rapids: Wm B. Eerdmans Publishing Company, 1958), pp. 39-40; Thomas Walter Manson, Studies in the Gospels and Epistles, ed. Matthew Black (Manchester: The Manchester University Press, 1962), p. 194.
[19] Munck, op. cit., pp. 141-142.

in terms of the later Gnosticism is to run the
risk of distorting the whole picture.[20]
In fact, Ridderbos states that recent archaeological
discoveries demonstrate that the Gnostic theory associated with the Christ party no longer has any credibility.[21] The theory assumes that second century Gnosticism was already developed in pre-Pauline days and
this assumption has not been proved.

I must conclude, therefore, along with Hans
Conzelmann that "since Paul does not enter into any
special opinions on the part of the groups, it is
impossible for specific positions which Paul combats
to be assigned to any specific group."[22] In other words,
we can conclude that the problem in the Corinthian
church is a concept, not a group of people. My point
is that Paul is instructing the Corinthian people
in eschatological living.[23] For this reason Paul addresses the Corinthian Christians as a unity. Paul
is concerned about the moral and religious disorders
which affect the whole Corinthian congregation. This
is evident from the diversions which characterize
the first four chapters; the serious case of immorality (chapter 5); the disapproval of seeking justice
from pagan judges (chapter 6); the question of marriage
(chapter 7); the questions regarding relationship
with the world (chapters 8-10); the proper administration of the Lord's Supper (chapter 11); spiritual
enthusiasm (chapters 12-14); and the resurrection

---

[20]"How Gnostic were the Corinthians?," New Testament Studies, XIX (October, 1972), 71. Wilson has given a solid criticism of this position also in his book Gnosis and the New Testament (Philadelphia: Fortress Press, 1968) and his review of Schmithals' Die Gnosis in Korinth in the Scottish Journal of Theology, XV (1962), 324-327. Consult also the criticisms of Conzelmann, A Commentary on the First Epistle to the Corinthians, pp. 14-16; Donald Guthrie, New Testament Introduction (Downers Grove: Inter-Varsity Press, 1973), pp. 422-423; Anthony C. Thiselton, "Realized Eschatology at Corinth," New Testament Studies, XXIV (July, 1978), 510-526; W. C. Van Unnik, Newly Discovered Gnostic Writings (Naperville: A. R. Allenson, 1960), p. 93; and Ridderbos, Paul, pp. 32-35. Though somewhat dated in light of newer discoveries, R. M. Wilson's work The Gnostic Problem: A Study of the Relations Between Hellenistic Judaism and the Gnostic Heresey (London: A. R. Mowbray, 1958) is still relevant.

[21]Ridderbos, Paul, p. 34.

[22]Conzelmann, op. cit., p. 14.

[23]Caution must be used here. Some scholars believe that Paul is attempting to rectify an abstract theological concept of eschatology such as "realized eschatology." This is the position

of the body (chapter 15). In other words, Paul is encouraging and demanding the Corinthians to submit to the sanctifying power of God in their lives (1:2, 30). Paul is instructing the Corinthians in exhibiting a faithful, obedient response to the work of Jesus Christ.

From this eschatological perspective we must take issue with Conzelmann's existential interpretation of Paul's address to the Corinthians. Conzelmann maintains that for Paul "theology is not an application of timeless principles but the understanding of the situation in which man finds himself at the moment in which grace reaches him through the word, he can therefore spotlight the church and the individual in the concrete position of the moment."[24] According to Conzelmann, the concrete situation of the moment dictates the application of Paul's theology. This cannot be true. Paul is not interested in whether the Corinthians can apply the word in the existential moment of a concrete situation; rather he presents an eternal principle which governs a given situation as well as any situation. This principle, based on the historical revelation of the Godhead, is eschatology. Paul approaches every moral and religious disorder in the Corinthian church from the eschatological viewpoint of life. The existential approach loses sight of how a governing principle of Paul's theology applies to a given situation. In fact, Conzelmann never mentions the concept of eschatology. His viewpoint limits Paul's "applied theology to the his-

of Nils A. Dahl, "Paul and the Church at Corinth According to I Corinthians 1-4," Christian History and Interpretation: Studies Presented to John Knox, ed. W. R. Farmer et. al. (Cambridge: At the University Press, 1967), p. 332; C. K. Barrett, A Commentary on the First Epistle to the Corinthians (New York: Harper and Row, Publishers, 1968), p. 109; F. F. Bruce, New Century Bible: 1 and 2 Corinthians (London: Oliphants, 1971), pp. 49-50; Ernst Käsemann, New Testament Questions of Today, trans. W. J. Montague (London: SCM Press LTD, 1969), pp. 125-126; and A. C. Thiselton, "Realized Eschatology at Corinth," 510-526. On the other hand, E. Earle Ellis points out that Paul is not trying to correct the theological rubric of eschatology (in abstraction), but is instructing the Corinthians in eschatological living. Ellis' position is set forth in his essay, "Christ Crucified" in Reconciliation and Hope: New Testament Essays on Atonement and Eschatology Presented to L. L. Morris on his 60th Birthday, ed. R. Banks (Exeter: The Paternoster Press, 1974), pp. 73-74.
[24]Conzelmann, op. cit., p. 9.

torical situation in Corinth." The principle of eschatology as Paul sets it forth, however, has no limitation. It applies to the Corinthian situation as well as to the entire period from the death and resurrection of Christ until His parousia, the prelude to the consummated state of the kingdom of God. As Thiselton writes: "Christians must strive to be now what they are to become."[25]

We have seen that Paul is concerned about the problem of eschatological living in the Corinthian church. In this context we must note, however, that although Paul does not address his letter to a party or faction, he does address his letter to a group of people identified as sarkinous or nēpiois (3:1). In Paul's estimation the people of the Corinthian church do not resemble a Christ-like maturity which is commendable to the Christian life. For this reason Paul addresses them as "men of flesh" or "babes in Christ" instead of "spiritual men." He has no concern for labeling the group Gnostics, Jewish, Gentiles, or Stoics; nor does he wish us to speculate about this. Paul is concerned about the Corinthian people as a unity, not about the individual bickerings of the party groups. Within the eschaton, the people as a whole have failed to live in the fulness of the benefits of the revelation and redemption of Christ. The phrases "men of flesh" or "babes in Christ" convey this failure. An understanding of the eschatological message of the gospel in Jesus Christ could alone bind the Corinthian factions together, i.e. bind them as "spiritual men."

We have now set the stage for the eschatological tension within the Corinthian church. This tension or antithesis between the "wisdom of the world" and the "word of the cross" becomes clear in Paul's use of the term sophia in I Corinthians. Paul's use of the word sophia (1:17-2:16) has, however, been the subject of debate. According to Ulrich Wilckens, most exegetes have understood that the term sophia in I Corinthians 1:18-2:5 is used by Paul to oppose the "philosophical or rhetorical presentation of the Gospel according to the standards of Greek philosophy."[26] Against this more traditional understanding, Wilckens believes that the term has the same significance through-

[25] Thiselton, op. cit., 517.
[26] Ulrich Wilckens, "Sophia: The New Testament," TDNT, VII, p. 522.

out 1:18-2:5 as well as throughout 2:6-2:16. Wilckens claims that Paul is not using the term *sophia* in order to reflect upon the theological aspects of Greek philosophy and theistic revelation, rather Paul uses the term *sophia* to confront a dispute related to the situation in Corinth. The situation, according to Wilckens, is that the Corinthian church has accepted a "Gnostically absolutised Pneuma-Christology."[27] Paul is addressing the problem of Gnosticism, not Greek philosophy. More specifically, Wilckens thinks that most likely the Christological ideas of the Corinthians were influenced by a synthesis of a Gnostic form of myth and the Jewish Sophia myth. In polemical and apologetic fashion, therefore, Wilckens claims that in I Corinthians 2:6-16, Paul "adopts the vocabulary and ideas of his opponents and is not afraid of the danger of using them in positive form as this is possible in the light of the preceding antithesis [wisdom of God/wisdom of the world] in 1:18-2:5. It is thus that we really learn what was understood by *sophia* in Corinth."[28] In Wilckens estimation, this is evident in what Paul writes in I Corinthians 2:6, 7: "Yet we speak wisdom among those who are mature; but not the wisdom of this age, nor of the rulers of this age, who are coming to nothing; but we speak the wisdom of God in a mystery, *wisdom* which has been hidden, which God foreordained before the ages to our glory." Wilckens claims that behind this text "stands the widespread Gnostic idea of the descent of the Redeemer through the zones of the archons, His [Christ's] true form being concealed from them and made known only to His own people who are redeemed by Him."[29] Wilckens states that this idea of descent is also clearly found in Jewish Gnostic Sophia myth. Here lies the synthetic element between the Gnostic myth and Jewish Sophia myth within Corinthian Christology. In Wilckens estimation, Paul had to confront this synthesis, and yet, in order to confront it he had to endorse the vocabulary and ideas of his opponents. In light of the Jewish tradition concerning disputes and arguments, therefore, Wilckens thinks it is logical that Paul would call the Corinthian position "Greek." It was Greek because it was a position foreign to the truth of revelation. Thus in Wilckens formulation, Paul uses the catchwords of his opponents (especially *sophia*) in order to call their position worldly wisdom. Wil-

[27] Ibid.
[28] Ibid., p. 519.
[29] Ibid., pp. 519, 520.

ckens believes that in this way Paul could more convincingly show that the Gnostic interpretation of the cross of Christ is foolishness.

C. K. Barrett holds to a viewpoint which emphasizes a varied use of the term sophia. As far as Barrett is concerned, sophia has a different shade of meaning every time it occurs in I Corinthians 1:19-2:16.[30] He states that this can be "grouped into two categories, good and bad, each with two subdivisions."[31] To begin with there is a group of passages in which sophia denotes "a kind of eloquence, a technique for persuading the hearer (1:17; 2:1; 2:4)."[32] It is a wisdom which relies upon a device of rhetoric. This kind of sophia, characterized by Barrett as dangerous (1:17; 2:1; 2:4), Paul refused to adopt when he first preached at Corinth. Barrett believes, however, that in 1:20 we observe one meaning of sophia moving into another. Here sophia "is more than technique; it has come to be a way of estimating and assessing life (cf. also 2:5, 13; 3:18-20)."[33] In summary, Barrett comments: "There is thus a sophia of speech, no bad thing (cf. 12:8), but dangerous; dangerous when preachers think they can use it as a substitute for Christ crucified, and most dangerous of all when it ceases to be human technique and becomes a humanistic philosophy."[34]

According to Barrett, there are two good uses of the term sophia in this section: 1) over against the sophia of the rulers (2:6) stands God's wise and mysterious plan for destroying the rulers and thereby freeing men from their authority. This use of sophia is essentially a Heilsplan; and 2) in 1:24, 30 we have the concept of Heilsgut in which Christ is sophia.[35] It is Barrett's position that these uses of sophia should enable the Corinthians to overcome both the sophia of rhetoric and a non-Christian assessment of life, and by so doing to become mature in spiritual living.[36]

[30] C. K. Barrett, "Christianity at Corinth," Bulletin of the John Rylands Library, XLVI (1964), 277.
[31] Ibid.
[32] Ibid., 278.
[33] Ibid., 278, 279.
[34] Ibid., 279. Barrett believes that the concept of sophia presented in 2:6 should also be included here (cf. 279, 280).
[35] Ibid., 281, 282.
[36] Though I have focused here upon the debate between Wilckens and Barrett, I must not fail to mention an important third posi-

In my estimation, the issue is not the various meanings of sophia nor the isolated situation which Paul addresses; rather, it is the meaning of sophia in redemptive history as it relates to the situation at Corinth. It is in this context that sophia describes the response of man to the revelation of God in Christ. The content of sophia, therefore, is to be understood in an antithetical manner.37 The all-inclusive content of sophia is either "the wisdom of the world" (the world and life view of "this present evil age") or the wisdom grounded in the ontological Godhead as He accomplishes His redemption in His people (the "age to come" becoming a present reality). Man's relationship with Jesus Christ is the definitive factor concerning which concept of sophia man finds himself. On the one hand, the unbeliever is part of the sophia of the world (1:20), the sophia of the age (1:20; 2:6). This sophia incorporates all unbelievers - Jews and Gentiles (1:22-24). Its content is dependent upon human resources (2:3), and thus, it is a description of a man who is merely a natural being (2:14). This man is perishing as well as his world because the content of his wisdom does not know God (1:21), and

tion in the debate, which is most challenging to both Wilckens and Barrett. This third position is held by those who believe that sophia must be understood in terms of Jewish wisdom literature, or, in more modern scholarship, Jewish apocalyptic wisdom literature. One of the earliest adherents of this position was Hans Windisch but it has come to expression in the modern debate in men like Günther Bornkamm, "Mystērion," TDNT, IV, P. 820; Birger Albert Pearson, The Pneumatikos-Psychikos Terminology in I Corinthians: A Study in the Theology of the Corinthian Opponents of Paul and its Relation to Gnosticism (Missoula: The Society of Biblical Literature, 1973), p. 33; Robin Scroggs, "Paul: Sophos and Pneumatikos," New Testament Studies, XIV (1967-1968), 35; Horsley, "Wisdom of Word and Words of Wisdom in Corinth," 224-239. I feel that they challenge Wilckens and Barrett because they guard the redemptive-historical significance of the term. In fact, Horsley, op. cit., 239, writes against Funk's isolated linguistic discussion that "Paul is concerned about historical-eschatological events, such as the crucifixion of Christ and the parousia, and about the eschatological community in its social-historical extension." Even this third group, however, fails because it makes Paul's term dependent upon apocalyptic presuppositions, instead of primarily upon the unique revelation of God as wisdom.

37 Consult especially the Greek construction of this contrast as set forth by Biörn Fjärstedt, Synoptic Tradition in I Corinthians: Themes and Clusters of Theme Words in I Corinthians 1-4 and 9 (Stockholm: Rotobeckman, 1974), p. 140.

thus, he interprets the <u>sophia</u> of God as foolishness (1:23; 3:19). On the other hand, we must understand <u>sophia</u> grounded in the ontological Godhead in the following way: God the Father, according to His eternal plan (2:7), has hidden His wisdom in a mystery (2:8). The mystery is the work of His Son, Jesus Christ (1:24, 30; 2:8). Christ's work is applied by the Holy Spirit (1:18) to those who are saved as the Spirit makes them wise in the ways of salvation (2:11-13).[38]

An all-inclusive understanding of Paul's use of the term <u>sophia</u> means that I do not hold that <u>sophia</u> has an abstract or isolated rhetorical reference in 1:17; 2:1,4 as Barrett does. This does not mean, however, that the gospel cannot fall prey to the wisdom of the world and be presented in a rhetorically clever manner hoping to persuade its audience on this basis (2:1,4).[39] But as far as Paul is concerned, his rhetori-

[38]This interpretation of <u>sophia</u> believes Barrett's theory of <u>Heilsplan</u> and <u>Heilsgut</u> interprets the word <u>sophia</u> too narrowly. For Paul the term in reference to God's wisdom is much more broad and yet more comprehensive in its meaning when it is seen as being grounded in the sovereign ontological Godhead as it comes to expression in the eschatological age. We must also say that Wilckens fails to understand the continuity of <u>sophia</u> because he has not comprehended the depth of the antithesis which Paul has constructed as it is redemptive-historically qualified. Paul is not thinking here of a Gnostic form of myth because he is thinking of all unbelief. Likewise, Paul cannot be incorporating a Gnostic form of myth in the Christian conception of <u>sophia</u> because he is opposed to such wisdom (cf. Robin Scroggs, op. cit., 33, 34 for further criticism of Wilckens' position).

[39]There has been some question as to whether the phrase "words of wisdom" in 1:17 has the same rhetorical connection with <u>sophia</u> as 2:1, 4. I do not think so. Endorsing the position set forth by Charles Hodge: "So far as the significance of these words (words of wisdom) is concerned, the meaning may be 1) not with skillful discourse, i.e. eloquence 2) or not with philosophical discourse, i.e. not in an abstract or speculative manner, so that the truth taught should be presented in a philosophical form. According to this view the doctrine taught would still be the gospel, but the thing rejected and condemned would be merely the philosophical mode of exhibiting it. 3) the meaning may be, not with a discourse characterized by wisdom; i.e. the contents of which was human wisdom, instead of truths revealed by God" (op. cit., pp. 17, 18). Because of the context, Hodge endorses the last interpretation mentioned, with which I agree. It is interesting that the New American Standard Version of the Bible endorses the first interpretation when it translates the

cal references to sophia in these texts (2:1,4) are a manifestation of the all-encompassing sophia of the world.[40] This is clearly evident when one does not isolate the rhetorical reference of sophia from the whole context of Paul's discussion (1:17-3:19).

Barrett would be, therefore, on firmer ground if he would drop the isolated rhetorical meaning of the term and strengthen his second understanding, the "way of estimating and assessing life." In this context Paul's point is that those who exist according to the wisdom of this world have a distinct world and life view. This world and life view stands in opposition to the revelation of the cross and under the judgment of the cross. The point, which is implicit in Barrett's position, is that the sophia of the world is a way of thought and existence which rebells against God. This sophia comes in various forms (e.g. Greek philosophy, Gnostic mythology of Christology, Jewish sects, the empire cult, etc.), but such a form represents the sophia of the world, the wisdom of unbelief. In I Corinthians 1:17-2:16 the various forms of unbelief come to expression in the Jewish community which asks for signs and in the Greek community which searches for wisdom. Although Paul mentions two specific groups in 1:22, he wants us to understand them as characterizing all mankind in their unbelief towards God (cf. 1:23). Thus we must understand the demand of Jew and Greek for signs and wisdom as the demand of fallen mankind before God.

How did the specific demand for signs and wisdom come to expression in the Jewish and Greek communities? The Jew demanded signs, but Paul preached Christ, who was a stumbling block to them. The message of a crucified Savior was repulsive to them because Deuteronomy 21:23 says that "he who is hanged is accursed of God." In light of their political aspirations, a crucified Messiah was an insult to their hopes for a Messiah

phrase as "cleverness of speech." This translation does not go well with the translation of logos and sophia throughout the rest of the text (1:17-3:23), where we find a much more literal translation of the Greek. In my estimation the NAV translation is inconsistent and confusing.

[40] Robin Scroggs, op. cit., 36, believes that the relationship between rhetoric and content of sophia in 1:18-2:5 is a "both-and" not an "either-or" proposition.

who would deliver and exalt their nation.[41] Paul realized, however, that the demand for these signs characterized the Jews since the call came to them to leave Egypt. It was evident even when they came face to face with Jesus himself (cf. Mt. 12:39; Mk. 8:11; Jn. 6:30). As Jehovah did in the Old Testament, Christ gave them many signs. Yet the Jews still rejected and despised Him, mainly because of their political aspirations and their legalistic view of the law. Because of this the Jews are reprobate and alien to Paul's gospel proclamation. They can even be said to be unteachable while they remain in this condition.[42]

In their search for wisdom the Greeks understood the message of the cross as foolishness. Why? First, as William Barclay brings out, the Greeks' viewed God's first characteristic as apatheia.[43] This word means more than just apathy; "it means total inability to feel."[44] The Greeks argued that God cannot feel such things as joy, sorrow, anger, or grief. If such emotions could affect God, they would have to be instigated by man, and thus, for that moment, man would be greater than God because he conditioned the mood of God. Thus the God-man Jesus Christ, who came to suffer, is a contradiction. The incarnation which led to Christ's suffering, therefore, made no sense to a Greek.[45] According to Greek philosophical presuppositions, Paul's position lacked logic and could not be true.[46] Secondly, the Greeks sought wisdom as it was expressed in speculative philosophy. Their great

---

[41] Jean Hering, brings this out in *The First Epistle of Saint Paul to the Corinthians*, p. 10: "For the Jews, on their side, a crucified Messiah was an insult to their messianic hopes, which were essentially political."

[42] cf. Calvin, *Institutes of the Christian Religion*, ed. John T. McNeill, trans. Ford Lewis Battles (Philadelphia: The Westminster Press, 1967), III. xxiv. 14., p. 981.

[43] *The Letters to the Corinthians* (Philadelphia: The Westminster Press, 1956), p. 20.

[44] Ibid.

[45] As Hering, op. cit., p. 10, states: "Why were the Greeks, or at least their philosophers, unable to believe in Christ curcified? The polemic of a Celsus or Porphyry shows us why: a God ignominiously condemned and executed could not be taken seriously ..."

[46] Hodge, op. cit., p. 23 comments: "To the Greeks this doctrine was foolishness. Nothing in the apprehension of rationality can be more absurd than that the blood of the cross can remove sin, promote virtue, and secure salvation; or that the preaching of that doctrine is to convert the world."

philosophers were the champions of their culture. These philosophers were not only great thinkers, but also, in later Greek culture, masters of rhetoric. The Greeks had become intoxicated with fine speech and by comparison viewed the message of Christian preaching as crude, uncultured, and ridiculous.[47]

It is evident that according to both the Jews and the Greeks "the idea that a man executed as a common criminal, suffering a degrading, humiliating death, could have anything to do with divine wisdom and salvation was utter folly."[48] Both groups demanded a proof of divine truth. In this way they set themselves up as an authority which could pass judgment upon God.[49] This attitude identifies them as worldly because it shows their way of thinking to be consistent with the "wisdom of this world." God is to subject Himself for proof to their criteria. But if God would subject Himself to their criteria, "revelation would have to present itself as a factor belonging to the world."[50] That, of course, is impossible for the God of the Scriptures, because revelation has its origin and completeness in this God as He makes Himself known in history. Paul clearly understood this fact. The "word of the cross" can never be preached with the same methodology and content as the "wisdom of the world." There is no accommodation of the preaching of the gospel to the ways of the world.

Paul preached Christ crucified because His crucifixion is a sign as well as wisdom to those who believe, to those who have submitted to God's revelation in His Son (1:24). The preaching of Christ crucified is a sign because it proclaims the triumph of the redeeming death and resurrection of Christ. Christ conveyed this in His own ministry. When the Jews asked Him for a sign, He pointed them to the tearing down and rising up of the temple, that is, to His death and resurrection (Jn. 2:18-22). This sign was

[47]cf. Barclay, op. cit., p. 22.
[48]Ladd, A Theology of the New Testament, p. 385.
[49]Conzelmann, op. cit., p. 47.
[50]Ibid. In this context Alan Richardson gives a damaging blow to Wilckens' theory when he states that Christ as "the power of God and the Wisdom of God cannot be understood in terms of Paul's incorporation of a mystical Gnostic sophia, because such wisdom is understood as foolishness with God. It is this kind of wisdom which the word of the cross is opposing." cf. An Introduction to the Theology of the New Testament (London: SCM Press LTD, 1958), p. 158.

nonsense to them, but it became the basis for the belief of His disciples. By preaching Christ crucified Paul has also proclaimed the incarnation of wisdom (1:20; 2:7, 8). This wisdom is life; it is a wisdom which has come in Christ and which reflects the eternal wisdom of the kingdom of heaven. By merely preaching Christ crucified, therefore, Paul is not presenting an abstract concept of the crucifixion; instead, he is preaching a powerful sign from God as well as the wisdom from God that is necessary for living in the eschatological bliss of redemption. It is a sign and a wisdom which the world does not know because it lives according to the "wisdom of the world."

In summary, redemptive history qualifies Paul's all-inclusive use of the concept *sophia* from 1:17 through 2:16. The term denotes either the "wisdom of the world," the way of unbelief conditioned by the Fall or the wisdom grounded in the Godhead who enlightens believers to the benefits of salvation. In both meanings, *sophia* describes the response of man to the preaching of the "word of the cross." Man's response to the message of Christ is either with the wisdom from man or with the wisdom from God. Though it is used as an all-inclusive term, it can also refer to specific groups of people such as Jews and Greeks. Even in this context, however, these specific references are part of the whole (1:20, 23, 24).

With the all-inclusive character of *sophia* established, I will develop for the remainder of this chapter what Paul means by his preaching of the "word of the cross" as it is antithetical to the "wisdom of the world." As Paul had preached and is now writing the "word of the cross" to the Corinthians, he was concerned that the situation of the Corinthians be understood in the context of the eschatological message of God. We find, therefore, the whole text bracketed by such eschatological concepts as the victorious preaching of the Messiah, the coming of the final Wisdom of God, the revelation of the mystery of God, the benefits of the Spirit of God poured out to man, and the judgment which comes upon the world. As far as our text is concerned, each of these concepts is intertwined with and dependent upon the other in conveying Paul's message to the Corinthians.

Scholars have stated that the unity of Paul's eschatological argument in I Corinthians 1:17-3:23 is exhibited in the six quotations from the Old Testament (1:19, 31; 2:9, 16; 3:19, 20). These quotations bear the same theme: "men cannot grasp God's wisdom through their own wisdom."[51] The message in this section, therefore, is not new. It is a message taken from the pages of the Old Testament, more specifically, from the wisdom and prophetic literature, in which God has already pronounced his judgment upon human wisdom (cf. Ps. 94:11; Jer. 9:23-33; Isa. 26:14). Paul warns the Corinthians that the Scriptures have always testified to the antithesis between the wisdom of the world and the wisdom of God. Never has God endorsed the wisdom of the world.

Although the theme of Paul's message is not new, there is one notable difference between the message of Paul and the message of the Old Testament: from Paul we learn that the wisdom of God has reached its fulfilled state in the person and work of Jesus Christ (cf. Prov. 8:12-36; I Cor. 1:30; 2:6-8). Here lies the eschatological unity of the six quotations from the Old Testament. Paul demands that the Corinthian church understand what God has done in the revelation of His Son. In the first place, He is the fulfillment of wisdom. Secondly, He comes judging the wisdom of unbelief (1:18), while on the other hand, He is the exalted wisdom of God (2:8). What was veiled in the Old Testament has now become a reality; what has been a mystery from the foundation of the world has now been made known (2:7). The mysterious wisdom of God, as He is being revealed, remains hidden from those who are perishing in this present evil aeon (1:18; 2:8). But for those who are being saved, the power and the wisdom of God are no longer a mystery (1:18, 24; 2:9).

Jesus Christ is the personification and incarnation of wisdom, who was ordained to come to redeem His people before the ages. He is Wisdom speaking in Proverbs 8, who has now appeared in the flesh on earth. As Wisdom, He has by virtue of His death, resurrection, and ascension become the righteousness (Prov. 8:18-20), the sanctification (Prov. 8:18-20, 30-34), and the redemption (Prov. 8:17, 35) of His

---

[51]Bartil E. Gärtner, "The Pauline and Johannine Idea of 'To Know God' Against the Hellenistic Background: the Greek Philosophical Principle 'Like by Like' in Paul and John," New Testament Studies, XIV (January, 1968), 216.

people (I Cor. 1:30).⁵² Jesus Christ is the final soteriological wisdom of God in service to His covenant people; He is the wisdom of the eschatological plan of His Father which is now being fulfilled (cf. also Eph. 1:10). The divine plan of creation, redemption, and consummation is fulfilled in Him. As far as Paul is concerned, the Corinthian church <u>must</u> grasp this fundamental truth which heals schism or prevents schism.

It is in this context, therefore, that Paul clearly understands the importance of preaching Jesus Christ alone through the power of the Holy Spirit. The Spirit, who is "brought into the eschatological era itself as forming the official equipment of the Messiah" (cf. Isa. 11:2; 28:6; 42:1; 59:21; 61:1)⁵³ has made known to Paul the mysterious wisdom of Christ, the "depths of God" (2:10), which have been hidden since the foundation of the world. He could preach, quite simply, but meaningfully, what he has come to know through the Spirit: "Jesus Christ and Him crucified" (2:2).⁵⁴ Although this may seem like a simple

---

⁵² In the <u>Institutes</u>, II. xv. 2., p. 496, Calvin says, "But when Paul says that He [Christ] was given to us as our wisdom (I Cor. 1:30), and in another place, 'In Him are hid all the treasures of knowledge and understanding' (Col. 2:3), he has a slightly different meaning. That is, outside of Christ, there is nothing worth knowing, and all who by faith perceive what he is like have grasped the whole immensity of heavenly benefits." In his commentary on <u>Corinthians</u> Calvin makes this conclusion: "Thus <u>redemption</u> is the first gift of Christ that is begun in us, and the last that is completed" (p. 94).

⁵³ Vos, "The Eschatological Aspect of the Pauline Conception of the Spirit," p. 218.

⁵⁴ Ridderbos makes a perceptive point of exegesis (<u>Paul</u>, p. 244), when he interprets the "depths of God" as synonymous with the "mystery of Christ." Thus, the Holy Spirit reveals the "mystery of Christ," i.e. the "depths of God." Such an interpretation brings out the genius of Paul's text, while the more traditional understanding of the deep things of God misses the whole point. This can be seen in Hodge, <u>An Exposition of the First Epistle to the Corinthians</u>, p. 39, who understands the "depths of God" to be the "inmost recesses, as it were, of His being, perfections, and purposes." Hodge then goes on to remark that "the Spirit, therefore, is fully competent to reveal that wisdom which had for ages been hid in God." In other words, according to Hodge, the Spirit is able to reveal the wisdom hid in God because He has access to the recesses of God's being, perfections, and purposes. Against this, Ridderbos, however, says that the Wisdom of God <u>is</u> the "depths of God."

statement, it nevertheless means the full-orbed eschatological message of the gospel. In his proclamation of the "word of the cross," Paul is declaring to the Corinthians that the only thing which has meaning for the life of the church, from creation to consummation, is Jesus Christ.[55] In other words, the preaching of Jesus Christ is the proclamation of the person and work of Christ as He is the eternal life of His people. The passage gives, therefore, no indication that Paul is limiting his message to an isolated idea of the crucifixion. By referring to the crucified Christ, Paul could remind the Corinthians of the suffering servant, while not forsaking the exalted and living Christ (1:17, 18, 30; 3:22). For Paul to preach Christ crucified is to preach the complete gospel (1:17), that is to include such important concepts as the obedience, the

[55] It is the position of some scholars that Paul here changes his method of preaching to the Corinthians because of his ineffectiveness at Athens (Acts 17). William Barclay clearly holds this position in The Letters to the Corinthians, p. 26: "It is worth noting where Paul had come from. He had come to Corinth from Athens. It was at Athens that, for the only time in his life, as far as we know, Paul had attempted to reduce Christianity to philosophic terms. There, on Mars' Hill, he had met the philosophers, and had tried to speak in their own language and to use their own terms and to quote their own authorities (Acts 17:22-31); and it was also there that Paul had had one of his very few failures. His sermon in terms of philosophy had had very little effect (Acts 17:32-34). It would almost seem that Paul had said to himself, 'Never again! From henceforth I will tell the story of Jesus in all its utter simplicity. I will never again try to wrap it up on human categories. I will know nothing but Jesus Christ, and Him upon His Cross.'" In agreement with this position are Marcus Dods, The Expositor's Bible: The First Epistle to the Corinthians (New York: Funk and Wagnalls Company, 1900), p. 53 and W. G. H. Simon, The First Epistle to the Corinthians: Creed and Conduct (London: SCM Press LTD, 1968) pp. 64, 65. We believe there is a competent reply to Barclay, Dods, and Simon by Alan Richardson, An Introduction to the Theology of the New Testament, p. 52: "Some commentators have suggested that it was the failure of his philosophical apologetic on the Areopagus that made Paul resolve that henceforward he would preach nothing but Christ and never again start from the 'wisdom of this world' (I Cor. 1:18-31). Such a suggestion is altogether unlikely. It is much more probable that Paul meant what he actually wrote to the Corinthians, namely, that his preaching of Christ was not a new mystery religion, a man-made sophia (I Cor. 2:1, 5f, 13), but a kerygma which, however foolish it might sound, was attested by the Holy Spirit of God. He is certainly not confessing that he had ever preached a man-made sophia,

death, resurrection and lordship of Christ.[56] This message proclaims the full plan of redemption which God the Father has ordained for His creation (2:6-8) as it is revealed by the power of the Holy Spirit (2:10-13). This is preaching the whole council of God.

In all of this, it is imperative to note that Paul himself does not determine the content of his preaching; rather, it has been fixed by the work of God. Jesus Christ, the mysterious Wisdom of God, goes to the cross to die for the salvation of sinners, because He submits to the eternal decree of His Father, and He is raised according to God's holy word so that sinners for whom He died will have eternal life.

at Athens or anywhere else; he is protesting that this is the one thing he could never do. Furthermore, it was not the rabbinic apologetic which had scandalized the Athenians; it was the idea of judgment and of a resurrection from the dead which they had mocked (Acts 17:32); it was the preaching of Christ crucified which appeared foolishness to the Greeks (I Cor. 1:23) ... There is no reason to doubt that in his summary of Paul's preaching on the Areopagus St. Luke has given us a faithful account of the kind of approach which St. Paul was accustomed to make to an audience of educated Greeks, whenever he had an opportunity to preach to them."

[56] Holmes Rolston, The 'We Knows' of the Apostle Paul (Richmond: John Knox Press, 1966) pp. 13, 14, ties Christ's suffering to His death and resurrection: "In our text he [Paul] says, 'We preach Christ crucified (2:2).' His statements sound very simple, but they have far-reaching implications ... Paul insisted that it was necessary for the Christ to suffer and die. He followed Jesus Himself in fusing the concept of the Messiah with the prophetic picture of the suffering servant. We can be sure that Paul told in Corinth the story of the life and death of Jesus. We can be sure also that he gave this witness to the resurrection. You cannot give the witness to the resurrection without first telling the story of the death of the Christ. But you cannot preach Christ crucified without moving on to the resurrection. You cannot call men to living faith in a dead Christ (cf. Rev. 1:17, 18; I Cor. 15:3-4). Paul gave in Corinth the testimony to the crucified and risen Lord." Hans Conzelmann, An Outline of the Theology of the New Testament, trans. John Bowden (New York: Harper and Row, Publishers, 1969), pp. 203, 204, points out that the resurrection is presupposed in Paul's preaching of the cross. Commenting on I Corinthians 1:17, 18, Ridderbos also speaks of the death and resurrection as inseparable from one another (cf. Paul, pp. 54, 55). In agreement with Conzelmann's view and adding to it the lordship of Christ is Bornkamm, Paul, p. 160.

God's redeeming work and the present proclamation of that work are inseparable; Paul's preaching proclaims the past redeeming acts of God because they are also the present redeeming events by which man is saved.[57] Paul's preaching is distinctively the eschatological message to the church,[58] a message so antithetical to the world that it is foolish to the world (1:18). God is pleased, however, to redeem His people through a foolish non-synthetic gospel (1:21).[59] Paul's preaching responds faithfully to the Father's providential plan of redemption; it proclaims Christ as the Lord of glory and submits to the power and work of the Holy Spirit. The whole accomplishment of redemp-

[57] For an adequate evangelical discussion of the relationship between content and meaning or event and proclamation, cf. Ladd, A Theology of the New Testament, pp. 387-388. This is an important discussion because there has been a tendency by modern New Testament scholars with their view of history to emphasize the proclamation of the "Christ-event" at the expense of the actual historical significance of the death and resurrection of Christ. A more radical approach is that which says that the proclamation of the "Christ-event" (mythically understood) only has meaning in terms of "existential decision" (cf. Rudolf Bultmann, Theology of the New Testament, I, p. 3).

[58] We believe that the first three chapters of I Corinthians are clear evidence that C. H. Dodd's definition of preaching is much too limited. In drawing a distinction between preaching and teaching in the New Testament, Dodd writes in The Apostolic Preaching and its Developments (London: Hodder & Stoughton Limited, 1936), p. 3: "Preaching, on the other hand, is the public proclamation of Christianity to the non-Christian world." Paul defines his whole commission from Christ, as a preacher. His preaching is not limited to non-Christians; it is also for the edification of believers. Paul's eschatological message as a preacher has no meaning unless it is applied to the believing church.

[59] God's purpose to save men through the "foolishness of preaching" refers to the content of preaching (Christ crucified; the cross), which is offensive and foolishness to all but believers (1:18, 21). Conzelmann brings this out in An Outline of the Theology of the New Testament, p. 241: "The folly lies exclusively in the content of the preaching, in the cross, which is preached as God's saving act." In his commentary on Corinthians, p. 46, Conzelmann adds: "Along with the preaching there immediately goes also the thought of the content, the cross. Preaching is not merely considered to be foolish; it is foolish, by God's resolve." Hodge, An Exposition of the First Epistle to the Corinthians, p. 21, also agrees: "The foolishness of preaching means the preaching of foolishness, i.e. the cross." cf. also Ladd, A Theology of the New Testament, p. 387.

tion, its plan, execution, meaning, and interpretation as it is preached by Paul, has its foundation in what God has sovereignly done, is doing, and will do. Paul's preaching is authoritative and unique because it submits completely to God's interpretation of redemptive history.

In preaching the whole eschatological message, Paul's preaching is asserting that the Holy Spirit transforms Christ's people into the Kingdom of heaven by ruling in their hearts, applying to the believer the benefits of a new existence in Christ. The faith of the believer grasps this new existence in Christ. This faith rests on the power of God's Spirit, not on human wisdom. The power of the gospel, therefore, delivers men who were once in darkness (those who were under the dominant wisdom of the world) into Christ's kingdom. This power overcomes the rule of Satan in man's life and produces a peace and holiness that only God can work, whether it be in a Jew or in a Greek (1:24). God's sovereign distribution of His powerful grace does not operate in terms of the world, exalting those who have the most knowledge, influence, and rank (cf. 1:26). God's grace works in those whom He calls, humbling them so that they boast only in Him (1:31).[60] The people of God find themselves in Christ not because they were wiser than

---

[60]Human pride and boasting are an affront to God. Conzelmann, An Outline of the New Testament, p. 243, points out what boasting in the Lord means in our text: "This boasting in the Lord is not, however, a new possibility inherent in being a Christian. It does not mean that the homo christianus can boast of his new wisdom. The emphasis lies onesidely on the en kyriō, on the 'not in me' (cf. I Cor. 4:7). Boasting in the Lord means boasting in the cross (Gal. 6:14)." Commenting on the non-human distinctions in the work of God's redemption, Ladd, A Theology of the New Testament, pp. 398, 543, writes: "The apostles, as the refuse of the world (I Cor. 4:13), are viewed by other men as something to be despised. The foolish, the weak, the low and despised in the world (I Cor. 1:27f) are men who came from the lowest social and cultural levels of human society ... The Church is a fellowship of the elect (Eph. 1:4; I Thess. 1:4), regardless of social status, education, wealth or race (I Cor. 1:27)," Hodge, op. cit., p. 25, tells us: "It is implied in this form of expression, which is repeated for the sake of emphasis, that is, on the one hand, the wise and the great were not chosen on account of their wisdom or greatness, so, on the other hand, the foolish and the weak were not chosen on account of their want of wisdom or greatness. God chose whom He pleased."

others but simply because God has chosen or called them (1:26-30).

I have noted that Paul believes that the "word of the cross" is not only the power of God in those in whom it has produced faith, but also that the power of His preaching is affected by the Holy Spirit. Paul instructs us even further concerning this latter idea. In 2:4, Paul states that he is not displaying in himself the spirit and power of preaching; rather the Holy Spirit and the power of God reveal themselves in his preaching, thus demonstrating the truth of his preaching.[61] The man of the world attempts to and succeeds in persuading people with worldly wisdom, but produces nothing. Paul, however, preaches the message of God, who comes down from heaven and works His power in the hearts of men.[62] As a consequence, his preaching produces much fruit. Paul can even point to the fact that God uses his personal defects to demonstrate the power of His Spirit (2:3). Paul relies therefore, not upon his skill of debate, persuasive speech, or human wisdom, but on the testimony which the Spirit bears to the truth. As Vos points out: "the theocentric bent of Paul's mind makes for the conclusion that in the Christian life all must be from God and for God and the Spirit of God would be the natural agent of securing this."[63]

In the eschatological age, the continual presence

[61] Grosheide, *Commentary on the First Epistle to the Corinthians*, p. 61. The noun *apodeixis* (which is found nowhere else in the New Testament) denotes proof or demonstration of some claim or fact, which comes to expression in the demonstration of God's power, which saves man and gives them new direction in life.
Concerning the word "power" in 2:4, some have taken it to mean miracles (cf. for example Calvin, *Institutes*, III, ii.35, p. 853), but the context points to what Hodge, op. cit., p. 32, says: "the demonstration of which the Spirit is the author, and which is characterized by power."
[62] Grosheide, op. cit., p. 62. According to Funk, *Language, Hermeneutic, and Word of God*, pp. 282, 283 the contrast of 2:4 is not between *peithos* (persuasion) and *apodeixis* (demonstration), but between demonstration and demonstration, word and word (1:24 and 1:30). It is also a contrast between wisdom and wisdom. Though I believe Funk to be on the right track, the contrast is more directly between the persuasive wisdom of the world and demonstrative wisdom of God.
[63] Vos, "The Eschatological Aspect of the Pauline Conception of the Spirit," p. 254. cf. also Calvin, *Institutes*, IV. xiv.

of the Holy Spirit governs and instructs the people of Christ. The Holy Spirit consecrates and molds them in the wisdom of Christ, making them temples in whom the Spirit dwells (3:16, 17; cf. also 6:19). Paul realizes that although the Holy Spirit is present in his preaching and in the lives of the Corinthians 2:12, 13, 16), they have not responded with equal maturity to the gospel of the cross. This, in essence, is the problem which Paul addresses in I Corinthians. The Corinthians have not fully apprehended what it means to live in the blessing and grace of the whole eschatological revelation of God as Paul preached it to them. As far as Paul is concerned, God has begun to fulfill His eschatological plan through the fulfilled plan of God, the cross of Christ, and the present work of the Holy Spirit which has transformed the life of the church into a supernatural and heavenly existence which is still struggling with the ways of the world. Nevertheless, there is no room in a church which has been transformed into a heavenly existence for schisms and bickerings. The environment of the church must be solely Christocentric, and thus, the church cannot substitute the wisdom of humans, or even human saints (1:12) for the Wisdom of God (3:22, 23). To do so is to live as the world lives (3:3).

Since the Corinthian church did not apprehend fully what it means to live in the whole eschatological revelation of God, Paul designates their problem as spiritual (3:1). The spiritual problem is made clear as Paul employs three terms which describe the Christian in relation to his response to the "word of the cross:" teleiois (mature; 2:6), pneumatikos (spiritual; 2:15), and sarkikos (fleshly; 3:3) or nēpiois (babes; 3:1).[64] In what way should these Christians be understood?

The teleioi, according to Paul, are sanctified Christians -- those who are mature, full-grown, perfect --they live eschatologically (1:30; 2:6).[65] They are

---

11., p. 1286, who sees all the work of God in the hearts of believers in terms of the illumination of the Spirit, not in terms of man's work (I Cor. 3:6-9).

[64] It is absolutely imperative in discussing these three terms we must have in mind not only the Corinthians' problem concerning eschatological living but also fundamental antithesis underlying this problem: the wisdom of this world versus the wisdom of God.

[65] Such a classification usually begins with the teleiois in 2:6; some refer to him as "a higher class of believer" (Conzel-

perfect because they are in Christ. Their perfection is not dependent upon a certain quality within their own natural being, rather it is dependent upon Christ, who is the source of love, faith, wisdom, moral integrity and knowledge in their lives.[66] Christ is the beginning and consummation of the believer's perfection. The issue is not whether absolute perfection can be attained here on earth. The point is that those who have been freed from the world and have been engulfed in Christ are perfect. The teleioi understand the full significance of the cross and live in that understanding. This is why Paul uses teleios as a general term for mature Christians.[67]

It can also be said on the basis of 2:6-16 that the perfect man is the spiritual man (pneumatikos). He is spiritual in contrast to the psychikos (natural) man, because the psychikos man cannot accept the things of God, whereas the spiritual man accepts the things of God because he has the mind of Christ. The spiritual man submits to the perfecting work of the Spirit.[68] Paul does not use, therefore, teleiois and pneumatikos

mann, A Commentary on the First Epistle to the Corinthians, p. 60), the Christian who belongs to a "higher sphere" (Meyer, Critical and Exegetical Commentary on the New Testament: Corinthians, p. 60), the Christian elite who receive a superior stage of Christian teaching (Hering, The First Epistle of Saint Paul to the Corinthians, p. 15), (Pearson, The Pneumatikos-Psychikos Terminology in I Corinthians, p. 28), and those few who are instructed with an "esoteric wisdom, which the congregation of Corinth do not even hear" (Scroggs, "Paul: sophos and pneumatikos," pp. 37, 38). All these viewpoints have classified the teleiois man as a superior Christian with respect ot the nēpiois. In my opinion this is completely out of character for Paul in this text and would defeat his whole cause. It would give Christians who are said to be superior an opportunity of boasting over against the "babes" in Christ. This is exactly what Paul is against in our text; he will allow no opportunity for boasting in a man (1:31) [cf. Paul Johannes Du Plessis, Teleios: The Idea of Perfection in the New Testament (Kampen: J. H. Kok, 1959), p. 180].

[66] Du Plessis, op. cit., p. 184.

[67] This is defended by Du Plessis, op. cit., p. 184 and by Gártner, "The Pauline and Johannine Idea of 'To Know God' Against the Hellenistic Background," p. 219.

[68] According to Vos ("The Eschatological Aspect of the Pauline Conception of the Spirit," p. 247), to belong to the world to come and to be spiritual are concepts which are interchangeable in Paul, because they both teach that the believer partakes of the mysteries of the future already.

as terms for two different persons in the church, but as characterizations of the Christians who live in the whole eschatological message of Christ. This distinguishes them from the world, which crucified the Lord of glory and lives according to its own spirit (2:8, 12).

When Paul introduces us to the sarkikos man (nēpioi; 3:1-3) in distinction from the teleioi man, he is not setting forth a classification of Christians in the church. Rather, "he sets himself against the religious immaturity of some."[69] Nevertheless, these distinctions enable Paul to address the specific spiritual problem of the Corinthian people. The problem is that they have responded to the "word of the cross" not as spiritually mature but as fleshly immature (3:1). They are acting like men of the world, allowing the flesh to be clearly evident in their lives. It is their immature way of life which motivates Paul to speak to them as "babes." As Ridderbos states: "it pertains to the wisdom given in Christ to proceed from immaturity to maturity. The church as a whole must be brought to 'all riches of the fulness of insight,' to the knowledge of the mystery of God, Christ, in whom are all the treasures of wisdom and knowledge hidden. Then will it no longer be thrown off its stride by specious fallacies and tossed to and fro and carried about by every wind of doctrine in the vain trickery of men (Col. 2:2ff; Eph. 4:13ff)."[70] Paul's desire is to see the Corinthian church living in the riches of Christ, not synthesizing the wisdom of the world with the wisdom of God.

In summary, although we can say that the sarkikos man is in the Spirit, he is not submitting himself to the full dominance of the Spirit. This is demonstrated by his jealousy and strife. Such a lifestyle is not and should not be part of the life of the church. Paul confronts this situation with a dogmatic Christocentric attitude which is both loving and firm. Paul has a compassionate understanding for the present eschatological struggle of the Corinthians, but he

---

[69]Ridderbos, Paul, pp. 436-437. It is probably now evident that I am against understanding the carnal man as a man before justification and therefore not a Christian. This is the position of George Baker Stevens, The Pauline Theology: A Study of the Origin and Correlation of the Doctrinal Teaching of the Apostle Paul (New York: Charles Scribner's Sons, 1911), pp. 299-300.

[70]Ridderbos, Paul, p. 243.

cannot condone their falling prey to the ways of the flesh, the wisdom of the world. They must not allow themselves to continue as sarkikoi, but must submit to the dominate power of the Spirit of God. Why should they do this?

In the first place, Paul wanted the Corinthians to realize that the wisdom of the world manifested itself in the "rulers of this age" (2:6-8), the secular and ecclesiastical rulers, who were responsible for the crucifixion of the Lord of glory.[71] The greatest example that the "wisdom of the world" is blind to

---

[71] Following the two solid reasons given by Leon Morris, The First Epistle to the Corinthians, pp. 54, 55, I support the position that the rulers of this age are earthly rulers: "The one is that throughout this passage Paul's contrast is between the wisdom and power of God as shown in the gospel, and the wisdom and power of man. To introduce now the thought of the wisdom of demonic powers is to bring in an extraneous concept. The other is that in vs. 8 it is princes of this world who crucified Christ in ignorance. The most probable understanding of this is of the Jewish and Roman leaders, all the more so since in Acts 3:17 the same word princes, archontes (there translated 'rulers') is used of them. It is also there said that they carried out the crucifixion in ignorance. By contrast the demons are explicitly said to have known who Jesus was (Mk. 1:24, 34). We conclude, therefore, that it is the temporal rulers that Paul has in mind." Those who also support this interpretation are: Grosheide, Commentary on the First Epistle to the Corinthians, p. 65; Simon, The First Epistle to the Corinthians: Creed and Conduct, p. 63; Ladd, A Theology of the New Testament, p. 435; Johannes Munck, Paul and the Salvation of Mankind, p. 156; Gene Miller, "Archontōn tou aiōnos toutou: A New Look at I Corinthians 2:6-8," Journal of Biblical Literature, XCI (December, 1972), 528; and Archibald Robertson and Alfred Plummer, A Critical and Exegetical Commentary of the First Epistle of St. Paul to the Corinthians (New York: Charles Scribner's Sons, 1929), p. 36. In this debate concerning the "rulers of this age," there are those who believe they are demonic powers: Conzelmann, A Commentary on the First Epistle to the Corinthians, p. 61; Hering, op. cit., pp. 16, 17; James Moffatt, The First Epistle of Paul to the Corinthians, pp. 29, 30; and Johannes Schneider, "stauros," TDNT, VII, p. 581. Still others hold to both interpretations, i.e. the phrase signifies both earthly rulers and the demonic powers which stand behind them: Cullmann, Christ and Time, p. 193; Pearson, The Pneumatikos-Psychikos Terminology in I Corinthians, p. 33; G. B. Caird, Principalities and Powers: A Study in Pauline Theology (Oxford: At the Clarendon Press, 1956), pp. 16, 17; and even the evangelical Vos, "The Eschatological Aspect of the Pauline Conception of the Spirit," p. 251.

the wisdom of God is found in those who under the dominance of such gross wisdom crucified the Christ. The point which Paul is urging the Corinthians to comprehend is that the wisdom of the world crucified their Christ. Clearly their lives should not reflect this kind of wisdom.

In the second place, the content of the wisdom of the world is clearly contrary to a theocentric way of thinking. It is wisdom resting upon human knowledge (2:5), a wisdom whose origin is in "the god of this world" (Satan; II Cor. 4:4), and which is therefore incapable of bringing man to God. This type of wisdom is distant from God and is fortified in its own autonomy against God.[72] Its world is a "self-contained life-context" which withstands God in its own wisdom.[73] This kind of wisdom is a mode of existence which dominates fallen man because of the curse of the Fall and which is moving him and his world to judgment and final destruction (1:18; 2:6). This kind of wisdom will never lead to a knowledge of God but away from it (3:19).

The content of the wisdom of this world is also pride. It measures God by its own standards. The result of this autonomous wisdom is that the unbeliever judges God's revelation of redemption as "folly" (1:23). In pronouncing a verdict of "folly" upon the revelation of God, he has brought God's verdict of condemnation upon himself (1:18). He who lives by the wisdom of the world, i.e. is part of the "present evil age," is a member of the kosmos (1:20, 21), and therefore, has no hope (1:18; 2:6). He is psychikos man who lives without the effectual benefits of the eschatological message of redemption proclaimed by Paul (2:12). He is incapable of receiving (ou dechetai) the message because he operates solely within the boundaries of his own thought.[74] The effect of sin in his heart has

---

[72]cf. Bornkamm, Paul, p. 159. As Raymond Bryan Brown, The Broadman Bible Commentary: I Corinthians, X (Nashville: Broadman Press, 1970), p. 303, writes: "The word wisdom in verse 21 [1:21] probably means man-centered wisdom the second time it is used. The wisdom of the world is human wisdom per se. It is false wisdom because it does not know God."

[73]Ridderbos, Paul, p. 92.

[74]Archibald Robertson and Alfred Plummer, op. cit., p. 49. Philip Edgcumbe Hughes, "Crucial Biblical Passages for Christian Apologetics," Jerusalem and Athens; Critical Discussions on the Theology and Apologetics of Cornelius Van Til, ed. E. R. Geehan (Philadelphia: Presbyterian and Reformed Publishing Com-

made him blind to the truth; he refuses to believe, to appreciate, or to obey. He is, therefore, unconverted and unregenerated. He is a man of the flesh (Rom. 8:9), devoting his life to the things of the <u>kosmos</u> rather then to the things of heaven.[75]

The <u>psychikos</u> man, moreover, can never judge the <u>pneumatikoi</u> man because the latter has already been redeemed and now waits for his glorification, whereas the <u>psychikos</u> man is perishing under condemnation. Paul's accusation is that by living like the world of the flesh the Corinthians are walking as mere men (3:3). They are walking in a wisdom which is autonomous, unspiritual and, therefore perishing. How can those who have been given the Wisdom of God want to be part of such rebellious wisdom? As God's fellow workers, the Corinthians must stand apart from the world. They are God's building (3:9), the temple of the Holy Spirit (3:16, 17), whose only foundation is Jesus Christ (3:11). This theocentric life of the Christian is antithetical to the wisdom of the world. The Corinthians must understand that it is the theocentric life which is destined for eternal bliss. Their union to their God must be clearly evident in their everyday life.

pany, 1971), p. 138, defends this understanding when he writes: "they are unable to discern the reality of the human situation, which also, of course, includes his own situation. But this incapacity is an incapacity of constitution; it is an incapacity of choice. He has chosen a lie instead of the truth, darkness instead of light, death instead of life."

[75]Traditionally it has been said that the <u>psychikos</u> man is the "animal man" or the "natural man" who depends upon the light of nature (Calvin, <u>Institutes</u>, II. ii. 20., p. 280), or belongs to nature because he is unconverted (Grosheide, <u>Corinthians</u>, p. 73, and Ladd, <u>A Theology of the New Testament</u>, p. 473). Calvin, <u>Corinthians</u>, p. 115, even says that he is natural man because he is "endowed with nothing more than the faculties of nature." Though there may be an element of truth to this traditional viewpoint concerning the natural man, it misses the eschatological context of Paul's writing. The issue is that the <u>psychikos</u> man is the non-eschatological man in respect to the blessings and grace of God's Wisdom. He belongs to the "present evil aeon" and all which that means.

Chapter 4

THE APOLOGETIC SIGNIFICANCE OF THE TWO AGES

Traditionally, evangelical-Reformed systematic theologians have placed eschatology at the end of their textbooks.[1] In our estimation this has damaged the uniqueness of Paul's theological framework. As we have demonstrated, Paul's entire theological framework is shaped by Christ coming eschatologically in the history of redemption. Paul's theology is simply and completely eschatological.[2] He always unites his eschatological stance in Christ with his theological task. Historically, systematic theologians have failed to take this unity into account. In their arrangement of theological loci (theology, anthropology, Christology, soteriology, ecclesiology and eschatology), these theologians have not grasped the significance of Pauline eschatology for their theological construction. This is clearly evident in Hodge and Berkhof. Hodge's discussion of eschatology is an isolated deliberation of the "state of the soul after death,"[3] whereas Berkhof focuses upon the ramifications of "individual eschatology" to the believer after death.[4] How could these men, who believe that the task of the systematic theologian is to arrange the revelation of God's written Word in a coherent and organic manner, miss eschatology as the key to comprehending the revelation of New Testament theology?

[1] Two examples stand out: Charles Hodge, Systematic Theology, III (New York: Charles Scribner's Sons, 1899), pp. 713-880, and Louis Berkhof, Systematic Theology (Grand Rapids: Wm. B. Eerdmans Publishing Company, 1972 [12th printing]), pp. 661-738.

[2] As Vos, Pauline Eschatology, p. 11, writes: "It will appear throughout that to unfold the Apostle's eschatology means to set forth his theology as a whole."

[3] Hodge, Systematic Theology, III, p. 713.

[4] Ibid., p. 667ff. He emphasizes individual eschatology even more in his condensed volume entitled the Manual of Christian Doctrine (Grand Rapids: Wm. B. Eerdmans Publishing Company, 1969 [10th printing]), pp. 333-361. In this volume he divides "The Doctrine of the Last Things" into two sections: "Individual Eschatology" and "General Eschatology." The former deals with physical death and the intermediate state whereas the latter deals with the second coming of Christ, the millenium and the resurrection, and the last judgment and the final state. It should not go unmentioned that Berkhof mentions the present historical meaning of the word eschaton, but he does not develop it (cf. Berkhof, Systematic Theology, p. 666).

The answer lies within the method of systematics: to present and defend logically the data of revelation which apply to the <u>individual's</u> journey of salvation from conception (natural theology or the existence of God) to consummation (the eschatological state after death). Systematics confines itself to a rational, scientific inquiry into the logical order of the believer's salvation (<u>ordo salutis</u>). In other words, systematic theology does not hold together by a historically revealed concept such as eschatology, but by a rational application of the <u>ordo salutis</u> to the individual. When Hodge argues, therefore, that "reason must judge the evidences of a revelation,"[5] there is more at stake than the idea that our faith and our theological doctrines must be founded upon sound reason. Hodge's comment also reveals the thought that reason is methodologically fundamental to the structure of systematics. This use of reason is based on Cartesian and Aristotelian logic.[6] Systematics applies the revelation of God rationally to the necessary assumption of personal existence: "I" (<u>cogito ergo sum</u>). The isolated "I" is, therefore, the starting point of the <u>ordo salutis</u>, in which the theologian applies isolated Biblical texts to the development of the Christian's life. Such a procedure inevitably places eschatology at the end of the textbook, because it reduces eschatology to the "last things" the believer receives in his redemption. Obviously,

---

[5] Hodge, <u>Systematic Theology</u>, III, p. 53.

[6] We know that Cartesian and Aristotelian logic had a strong influence upon the Reformed thought and method of Francis Turretin, whose work <u>Institutio Theologiae Elencticae</u> (3 volumes, 1679-1685) was the textbook for the Princeton theologians(Alexanders, Miller, Hodges) and their students. We find in Turretin the beginnings of a return to scholastic-Aristotelian thought in the manner in which he views the autonomy and sovereignty of the liberal sciences. In fairness to him, however, it should be noted that Turretin denies that theology is a science in the sense of Aristotle's definition. In this he follows the Epicurean atomism of his teacher Pierre Gassendi. For Turretin theology is really <u>sui</u> <u>generis</u>. We should also point out that he studied under and was influenced by Marie Schurman, who was within the circle of Descartes. Though we find only the seeds of Aristotelian and Cartesian thought in Francis Turretin, they blossom fully in the thought of his son, Jean-Alphonse Turretin, who also influenced Reformed thought. For an excellent presentation of the two Turretin's theology see John Walter Beardslee, <u>Theological Development at Geneva under Francis and Jean-Alphonse Turretin</u> (1648-1737) (Ann Arbor: University Microfilms, Inc., 1956).

therefore, the historical nature of God's redemptive revelation is not primary in traditional systematics; rather, the individual's history is primary as the revelation of God sovereignly redeems him. This rationalistic method begins with man as the given in the theological procedure, instead of beginning with the self-attesting God of the Scriptures, who has revealed Himself in redemptive or covenantal history.

The starting point of Cornelius Van Til's theological method is opposed to this rationalistic method. The uniqueness of Van Til's theological method is that it begins by presupposing the self-attesting God of the Scriptures. He begins his discussion of systematic theology by saying that "fundamental to everything orthodox is the presupposition of the antecedent self-existence of God and his infallible revelation of himself to man in the Bible. Systematic Theology seeks to offer an ordered presentation of what the Bible teaches about God."[7] Van Til's definition of systematic theology unfolds in at least two directions. The first direction offers an "ordered presentation of what the Bible teaches about God." His syllabus on systematic theology, for example, begins by discussing the method of systematics which presupposes the ontological Godhead, and then it proceeds to "Christian Epistemology." It finishes with the "communicable attributes of God." The second direction reveals that systematics serves as the starting point of a Reformed-evangelical apologetic.[8] According to Van Til, systematics must precede apologetics: <u>what</u> we defend must precede <u>that</u> we defend.

In describing what is Reformed theology, Van Til presents what the Bible teaches about God and His relationship with man, using the traditional rubrics of systematics (doctrine of God, doctrine of man, doctrine of Christ, doctrine of the Church, doctrine of salvation, doctrine of the last things.)[9] Obviously Van Til does not see the necessity to challenge the traditional order of the rubrics of systematic theology. Instead, his concern is to present and defend a theology which begins with the self-

[7] Cornelius Van Til, <u>An Introduction to Systematic Theology</u> (Philadelphia: Class Syllabus, 1970), p. 1.
[8] Both <u>The Defense of the Faith</u> (Philadelphia: Presbyterian and Reformed Publishing Company, 1967), pp. 7-22, and <u>Apologetics</u> (Philadelphia: Class Syllabus, n.d.), pp. 4-22, by Van Til, already testify to this.
[9] cf. <u>The Defense of the Faith</u>, p. 9; <u>Apologetics</u>, p. 4.

attesting, sovereign God of the Scriptures rather then with man. His presentation and defense of Christian theology refutes, therefore, his Princeton Reformed brethren (the Hodges, Warfield, and others), as well as Arminianism and Catholicism at their respective starting points. Contrary to their views, Van Til emphasizes the need to grasp a proper understanding of the Creator-creature relationship in our theology. In other words, Van Til's primary concern is to present a correct view of the Creator-creature relationship within the traditional rubrics of systematic theology. For example, concerning the loci of eschatology, Hodge remains faithful to his method, examining and setting forth the concept of eschatology in a rational and individualistic manner, whereas Van Til discusses eschatology in terms of God's sovereign control of the future.[10] In other words, Hodge focuses upon the individual blessing the believer receives from God after death, whereas Van Til focuses upon the idea that the believer submits to the fact that the future is always shaped and interpreted by our sovereign God.[11] In a brief discourse on eschatology,[12] Van Til attempts to give a correct understanding of this doctrine in terms of the Creator-creature distinction. He believes that Hodge failed to accomplish this.

Although Van Til develops each topic of systematics within the scope of a proper Creator-creature distinction, he nevertheless does not challenge the order of the various rubrics. For him, therefore, eschatology concerns only the future, just as it does for Hodge and Berkhof. Why has Van Til failed to question the traditional sequence of the <u>ordo salutis</u>? I think there are two answers.

In the first place, it is important to note briefly Van Til's view of rationality and his theory of knowledge. According to Van Til, "God is absolute rationality. He was and is the only self-contained whole, the system of absolute truth. He is self-contained rationality. His rationality is not something he possesses, but is something with which His

[10] Van Til, in his <u>Defense of the Faith</u>, pp. 20, 21, writes that the Christian "believes that God has interpreted the future; he believes that the future will come to pass as God has planned."
[11] Ibid., p. 21.
[12] In both places where Van Til discusses the topic with regard to systematic theology, he gives only two paragraphs to the subject: cf. <u>Apologetics</u>, p. 22, and <u>Defense of the Faith</u>, pp. 21, 22.

being is coterminous."¹³ In other words, "He (God) cannot refer to rationality as something beyond Himself in order to distinguish Himself as rational. God does not possess rationality; He is rationality."¹⁴ According to Van Til, in a truly Christian system there is no abstract or neutral concept of reason distinct from God's Being. If there were, reason would of necessity be self-contained and self-sufficient without God. Thus, for Van Til God as rationality is self-contained only within God. Likewise, God's knowledge of Himself is not gained; nor is it dependent upon reference to anything that exists outside of Himself. God's knowledge of Himself is, therefore, self-dependent and completely coherent within Himself. Van Til calls this the <u>analytical</u> aspect of God's knowledge and rationality. Man's reason and knowledge, on the other hand, are derived from God and are reinterpretations of God's rationality and knowledge. That is, man's reason and knowledge are <u>analogical</u> to God's rationality and knowledge. It is necessary, however, to remember that according to Van Til's concept of analogy, man's reason and knowledge are entirely subordinate, finite, and temporal; they can never equal the eternal and infinite wisdom of God. To clarify this point "man, using his tools of reason and logic [law of contradiction] in subordination to the revelation of God was and is to reconstruct a finite replica of God's knowledge, 'when we speak of our concept or notion of God, we should fully be aware that by that concept we have an analogical reproduction of the notion that God has of himself. Our notions or concepts are finite replicas of God's notions.'"¹⁵

Van Til's view of man's rationality as analogical to God's reason forms the basis of his theological method. He presents the content of each theological heading as a finite replica of God's infinite rationality. When Van Til uses the tools of reason and logic within their true bounds, he believes that it is necessary and proper for the Christian to "systematize the facts of revelation."¹⁶ Van Til chooses to systematize God's revelation according to the tradi-

---

¹³<u>Systematic Theology</u>, pp. 10, 206.
¹⁴Jim S. Halsey, <u>For A Time Such As This: Introduction to the Reformed Apologetic of Cornelius Van Til</u> (n. p.: Presbyterian and Reformed Publishing Company, 1976), p. 18.
¹⁵Halsey, op. cit., p. 50. The quote within this quote is from Van Til, <u>Systematic Theology</u>, p. 206.
¹⁶Van Til, <u>Systematic Theology</u>, p. 11.

tional order of systematics. In doing so, however, he concentrates so much upon a proper view of analogy with respect to the content of each topic that he fails to question its traditional order.

Should the concept of analogy be applied only to a correct formulation of the Creator-creature relationship within the content of the topics of systematics? Is it not true that the rationality of God is also revealed to man in the process of history? In a rare point of weakness, Van Til does not follow through with the implications of his thought at this point. If the Christian uses the tools of reason and logic correctly in subordination to the revelation of God, is it not imperative that he follow the historical structure of God's revelation of Himself when he constructs a finite replica of God's knowledge? It is clearly evident to me that if man is to acquire a proper rational formulation of God's knowledge, he must submit to the manner in which God rationally reveals Himself to man. God has made Himself rationally understandable through the progressive revelation of Himself in redemptive history. Van Til simply fails to apply his concept of analogy to the historical process of God's revelation, and therefore, we can understand why he fails to correct the order of the traditional topics of systematics. For our theological task to be truly analogical, it must be organized in submission to God's organic plan of redemption revealed to us in His Word. In other words, the ordo salutis is subordinate to the historia salutis.

The second reason why Van Til fails to critique the traditional sequence of the ordo salutis is his failure to grasp the significance of the place he gives to biblical theology. Following the thought of his most influential teacher, Geerhardus Vos, Van Til places biblical theology before systematic theology.[17] He writes:
> Biblical theology takes the fruits of the exegesis and organizes them into various units and traces the revelation of God in Scripture in its historical development. It brings out the theology of each part of God's Word as it has been brought to us at different stages, by means of various authors. Systematic theology then

[17] cf. Geerhardus Vos, Biblical Theology: Old and New Testaments (Grand Rapids: Wm. B. Eerdmans Publishing Company, 1948), pp. 11-27.

> uses the fruits of the labors of exegetical and biblical theology and brings together into a concatenated system.[18]

To my knowledge, this is the most comprehensive statement in Van Til's writings concerning the relationship of biblical theology to systematic theology. To enhance our understanding of the above quotation, one should consult Van Til's close friend and colleague, Professor John Murray.

Like Van Til, Murray's interest in the relationship between biblical and systematic theology resulted from Vos' influence upon his exegetical thought. Murray writes that "only when systematic theology is rooted in biblical theology does it exemplify its true function and achieve its purpose."[19] Why? For these reasons:

> Systematic theology deals with special revelation as a finished product incorporated for us in Holy Scripture. But special revelation in its totality is never properly conceived of apart from the history by which it became a finished product. As we think of, study, appreciate, appropriate, and apply the revelation put in our possession by inscripturation, we do not properly engage in any of these exercises except as the panorama of God's movements in history within our vision or at least forms the background of our thought. In other words, redemptive and revelatory history conditions our thought at every point or state of our study of Scripture revelation. Therefore, what is the special interest of biblical theology is never divorced from our thought when we study any part of Scripture and seek to bring its treasures of truth to bear upon the synthesis which theology aims to accomplish...when systematic theology is consciously undertaken with the claims and results of biblical theology in view, then the perspective gained is more than that merely of unity. It is the unity of a growing organism that attains its fruition in the New Testament and in the everlasting covenant ratified and sealed by the blood of Christ.[20]

[18]Systematic Theology, p. 2. cf. also Apologetics, p. 3.
[19]John Murray, "Systematic Theology," The New Testament Student and Theology, ed. John H. Skilton, III (n. p.: Presbyterian and Reformed Publishing Company, 1976), p. 30.
[20]Ibid., pp. 30, 31.

Clearly according to Murray and Van Til systematics must conform to the redemptive-historical process of revelation as it is presented in God's Word (biblical theology). If this concept is correct, and I believe it is, salvation must be accomplished and applied by the sovereign work of the ontological Godhead in history. Redemption must be understood in terms of the historia salutis, and any formulation of the logical order of salvation (ordo salutis) must be constitutive of the historia salutis. As one can see, such a conclusion concerning the relationship between systematics and biblical theology is ultimately futile unless it is applied to the sequence of the rubrics of systematics.

Even Van Til and Murray ultimately fail to make this application. Van Til falls into the danger that Murray feared in systematics, i.e. the "tendency to abstraction,"[21] or more pointedly a "tendency to dehistoricize, the tendency to arrive at 'timeless formulations' in the sense of topically oriented statements which do not adequately reflect the fact that God's self-revelation (verbal communication) is an integral part of the totality of his concrete activity in history as sovereign creator and redeemer."[22] Being unaware of the final implications of his thought, Van Til's focus upon correcting the content within the topics of systematics by his concept of analogy remained an abstract formulation. Van Til never really placed the topics of systematics totally within the concrete activity of our sovereign God in history. The second reason, therefore, that Van Til does not question the traditional sequence of the ordo salutis is his failure to comprehend the implications of his formulation of systematic theology as they apply to biblical theology. He was able to correctly question the traditional rational and individualistic method in Reformed theology, but he does not thoroughly uproot it.

Murray also fails to apply his ideas concerning the relationship of systematic theology and biblical theology to the traditional construction of the ordo salutis. Why? To answer this we must realize that Professor Murray was a serious proponent of traditional

[21] Ibid., p. 30.
[22] Richard B. Gaffin, Jr., "Systematic Theology and Biblical Theology," The New Testament Student and Theology, III, (n. p.: Presbyterian and Reformed Publishing Company, 1976), p. 43.

Reformed systematics. Typical of late nineteenth-century and early twentieth-century Reformed systematics, therefore, Murray speaks of the accomplishment of redemption in Christ almost exclusively in terms of the atonement.[23] The first sentence of his work, Redemption: Accomplished and Applied, reads: "The accomplishment of redemption is concerned with what has been generally called the atonement."[24] In this statement we note that Murray does not mention the resurrection of Christ as part of His redemptive work. This seems mysterious, since the resurrection is so central to Geerhardus Vos, his teacher, for understanding New Testament theology. This failure permits him to by-pass eschatology in the accomplishment and application of redemption in Christ.

In the section on the application of redemption, therefore, Murray endorses the traditional structure of the ordo salutis, taking the believer on his individual journey from beginning (effectual calling as the initial step) to consummation (glorification as exclusively future).[25] As far as the relationship of biblical theology to systematic theology is concerned, Murray believes that the historia salutis is the foundation of the ordo salutis. Although he holds this position, he nevertheless does not challenge the traditional structure of the ordo salutis in light of the historia salutis; he exposits the redemptive-historical work of Christ in the traditional manner, i.e., in terms of the accomplishment and application of the atonement to the individual believer.

It would finally take a student of Van Til and Murray, Richard B. Gaffin, Jr., to consistently apply the proper relationship of biblical theology to systematic theology, as expounded by Vos. Maintaining the position of Vos and Ridderbos, Gaffin points out that "the center of Paul's teaching is not found in the doctrine of justification by faith or any other

[23]Gaffin briefly traces the place of the Reformed doctrine of the atonement in this period in The Centrality of the Resurrection, p. 12n.

[24]Redemption: Accomplished and Applied (Grand Rapids: Wm. B. Eerdmans Publishing Company, 1955), p. 9.

[25]Murray, Redemption: Accomplished and Applied, pp. 88-181. Ridderbos, Paul, p. 14, traces this traditional formulation of the ordo salutis in pietism, mysticism, and moralism all of which emphasized the "process of individual appropriation of salvation given in Christ."

aspect of the ordo salutis. Rather, his primary interest is seen to be in the historia salutis as that history has reached its eschatological realization in the death and especially the resurrection of Christ."[26] Gaffin goes on to observe, again in agreement, that the second chapter of Vos' Pauline Eschatology entitled, "The Interaction between Eschatology and Soteriology" "is an implicit rejection of the notion that the ordo salutis as traditionally conceived or a particular aspect thereof, is Paul's central interest. Rather he views the present soteriological realities of the believer's experience out of a broader eschatological perspective and as themselves the realization of the eschaton."[27] Unlike Van Til and Murray, Gaffin sees what this means:

> If there is one conclusion that a redemptive-historically sensitive interpretation of Scripture has reached [if you will, biblical theology] it is that eschatology is to be defined not only with reference to the immediate state of individuals following death and to the second coming of Christ but as also inclusive of His first coming and the present existence of the church in the world. This is an insight of a magnitude that requires recasting not only eschatology but also the other loci as traditionally conceived [systematic theology], especially Christology, soteriology, both accomplished and applied, and ecclesiology.[28]

At this point Gaffin applies Van Til's transcendental method to the traditional structural concept of the rubrics of systematics.[29] He realizes as Vos

---

[26] Gaffin, The Centrality of the Resurrection, p. 13.
[27] Ibid.
[28] Gaffin, "Systematic Theology and Biblical Theology," pp. 49, 50.
[29] This is the first time I have used the phrase "transcendental method" to represent Van Til's position as opposed to the traditional method. In his "Response by C. Van Til to Herman Dooyeweerd," Jerusalem and Athens: Critical Discussions on the Theology and Apologetics of Cornelius Van Til, ed. E. R. Geehan (n. p.: Presbyterian and Reformed Publishing Company, 1971), p. 98, Van Til defines the method in relationship to apologetics. This definition, however, applies basically to the whole spectrum of theology. For example, as applied to theology, it means we must accept the authority of God in His word in order to perform our theological task. And one must understand the biblical concept of analogy if theology is to be carried out correctly. Gaffin abides within these principles.

does that God is "the source and the end of all that exists and happens."[30] Jesus Christ is the Alpha and the Omega (Rev. 1:8). Eschatology, the doctrine of the last things, must be understood as part of the complete revelation of Christ. In Christ that which was seen to come last is actually first and last. Since God has brought forth His sovereign plan of redemption in His Son, a Christocentric eschatology cannot be the last rubric of Christian theology; rather, it must be the formal beginning as well as the permeating force throughout Christian theology.[31] In such a scheme the life of the believer is not presented as an isolated personal journey of salvation from the conception of his individual faith to its consummation. Rather, the individual's existence is defined from beginning to end in terms of his unity

[30]Vos, Pauline Eschatology, p. 61. One of the problems with some of the modern liberal scholars is that they understand God as only future, as the end. There is little said that God is the beginning because in their view the beginning is swallowed up by the end. This is seen in the title and content of John A. T. Robinson's work In the End God (New York: Harper and Row, Publishers, 1968).

[31]One may raise the issue that some liberal scholars have also stated that eschatology is the starting point of the systematic textbook instead of its end. For an example of this see Wolfhart Pannenberg, "Introduction," and his article "Dogmatic Theses on the Doctrine of Revelation," in Revelation as History, ed. Wolfhart Pannenberg, trans. David Granskou (New York: The MacMillan Company, 1968), pp. 1-19, 123-155; Jürgen Moltmann, Theology of Hope: On the Ground and the Implications of a Christian Eschatology, trans. James W. Leitch (New York: Harper and Rows, Publishers, 1967), pp. 15-19; and Gerhard Sauter. Zukunft und Verheissung: Das Problem der Zukunft in der gegenwartigen theologischen und philosophischen Diskussion (Zurich: Zwingli Verlag, 1965). For an excellent chapter on the subject consult Klaus Koch, "Systematic Theology Turns to Eschatology," The Rediscovery of Apocalyptic, pp. 98-111. How does my position differ from the liberal formulation? There are many differences but allow me to state some salient ones: 1) their view stands or falls with the incorporation of apocalyptic literature's view of eschatology into Christian theology; 2) their formulation does serious damage to the eschatological plan decreed and carried out by the sovereign God of heaven and earth; 3) according to Pannenberg revelation does not occur by a direct revelation of God in history; 4) eschatology for Moltmann ends as a revolutionary ideology which brings cosmic redemption to mankind; and 5) both Moltmann and Sauter fail to understand the present significance of Christ's death and resurrection for eschatology. For them eschatology has almost an exclusive future significance.

with the death and resurrection of Jesus Christ in history.³² In this biblical formulation, the individual believer can never legitimately focus upon himself, upon the I, with respect to his salvation; rather, one is always driven to God's sovereign work in history. If there is any necessity for an <u>ordo salutis</u>, then it must be understood as constituted by <u>the historia salutis</u>. In line with Vos and also drawing upon the work of Van Til and Murray, Gaffin has uprooted the traditional rational and individualistic method. In place of that method he has presented a consistent transcendental method with respect to Christ's saving work in history. Eschatology now has its proper biblical position in the encyclopedia of theology.

The stage is now set for the position of apologetics in the encyclopedia of theology. Being in agreement with Van Til, who places apologetics after exegesis, biblical theology, and systematic theology, I reconstruct the scheme as follows: exegesis (hermeneutics), theology as eschatology, and apologetics.³³ Apologetics must, therefore, presuppose hermeneutics since it unfolds the means by which we are to interpret and understand the message of the Scriptures. Apologetics must also presuppose the content of the biblical message (theology as eschatology). One cannot defend the biblical message of Christianity unless one has that content firmly intact: the <u>what</u> (content) precedes the <u>that</u> (defense). Both hermeneutics and theology as eschatology must serve as the <u>prolegomena</u> to Christian apologetics. In this context, apologetics "seeks to defend the eschatological system of

---

[32] cf. Gaffin, <u>The Centrality of the Resurrection</u>, pp. 114-127, and Vos, <u>Pauline Eschatology</u>, pp. 42-61.

[33] All I have said thus far in this chapter allows me to conclude with Gaffin, "Systematic Theology and Biblical Theology," p. 49, that "this prompts the not entirely modest proposal, in view of objections that can be raised against the term 'systematic theology,' to discontinue its use and instead to use 'biblical theology' to designate the comprehensive statement of what Scripture teaches (dogmatics), always insuring that its topical division remain sufficiently broad and flexible to accommodate the results of the redemptive-historically regulated exegesis on which it is based. This, it would seem to me, is the ultimate resolution of the relational question raised in this essay" (p. 49). At this time I should note that Gaffin is not an apologist, but a New Testament scholar. My dependence upon his work is not because he addresses apologetic issues, but because he provides insight into the position of apologetics in the theological spectrum.

biblical truth against false philosophy and false science."[34]

If one is going to defend the eschatological system of biblical truth, it will be accomplished in the context of the two age construction. Apologetics defends the "age to come" against the falseness of the "present evil age." The first duty of apologetics, therefore, is to instruct the Christian (who belongs to the "age to come") in defending the fulness of time against those who belong to the "present evil age." For this reason it is clear that the first duty of apologetics can never be the demonstration of theism.[35] The Christian view of theism must be presupposed because it has already been established in hermeneutics and in theology as eschatology. The foundation of a biblical apologetic is the sovereign ontological Godhead and His direct revelation in eschatological history instead of beginning with the rational faculty of man. This is not to say that our procedure is irrational or that it surrenders the analytical function. On the contrary, on the basis of the revelation of God, the presupposition of the sovereign ontological Godhead and His direct revelation in eschatological history is the only logical way in which to proceed. The traditional approach believes that reason is the all-inclusive human principle which judges and organizes revelation into a complete theological and philosophical system. On the other hand, I believe that the historical revelation of God, recorded in His self-attesting Scriptures, is the all-inclusive principle which organizes the logical proce-

[34] I have taken here the definition of apologetics that Van Til gives (Systematic Theology, p. 2) and inserted the word "eschatological" to serve my purpose.

[35] I am thinking here of the more traditional method of apologetics found in such works as William Paley, Natural Theology, (Boston: Gould and Lincoln, 1859); Hodge, Systematic Theology I, pp. 191-441; Bishop Joseph Butler, The Analogy of Religion, ed. Joseph Cummings (New York: Phillips and Hunt, 1884), pp. 45-190; George P. Fisher, The Grounds of Theistic and Christian Relief (New York: Charles Scribner's Sons, 1892), pp. 1-102; Professor Robert Flint, Theism (New York: Charles Scribner's Sons, 1909); Stuart Cornelius Hackett, The Resurrection of Theism: Prolegomena to Christian Apology (Chicago: Moody Press, 1957); Floyd E. Hamilton, The Basis of Christian Faith: A Modern Defense of the Christian Religion (New York: Harper and Row, Publishers, 1964), pp. 1-120; and John H. Gerstner, Reasons for Faith (Grand Rapids: Baker Book, 1967), pp. 23-57.

dure of a complete theological and philosophical system. In this construction reason operates within the structure of revelation as a component of revelation, and thus, reason serves as an aid to critique any procedure which is not congruent with a Christian universe.

As the apologist proceeds, he may wish to include a demonstration of theism, but it is not the first duty in apologetics. The Christian must always begin his apologetic by grasping the sovereign plan of God's revelation in the history of redemption as it has its focal point in the person and work of Jesus Christ. It is the person and work of Christ and our unity with Him that provides the present eschatological scheme of our apologetics. God's gracious gift of redemption in Christ has separated us from the kosmos (present evil age), and thus, the antithetical boundaries of the believer's apologetic task are firmly established in the two ages. By being separated from the present evil age by God's grace, the apologist must begin by understanding that he is defending a holistic system of thought, i.e. all that the fulness of time means, over against the various non-Christian holistic systems of thought. This means that a Christian apologist can never begin his analysis and critique of a non-Christian system of thought by focusing upon what both systems of thought have in common since both systems of thought are antithetical of each other.

Thus, the Christian two age apologetic defends the all-inclusive Kingdom of heaven, the Wisdom of God, the ways of the Spirit, and the full-orbed eschatological message of the gospel (age to come) against the all-inclusive Kingdom of Satan, the wisdom of the world, the ways of the flesh, and the foolishness of unbelief (present evil age).

As I have stated, the believer must understand his total identity in terms of his union with the saving eschatological work of God. According to Paul, the believer's union with Christ is defined by the redemptive-historical period in which he lives. He lives in the period between the resurrection of Christ and His second coming, i.e. the beginning ("already") of eschatological existence and the consummation ("not yet") of this existence. In such a structure the believer must not primarily view his existence in terms of his own time in history. Instead, he must analyze and critique all non-Christian thought within the scope of God's present eschatological boundaries (death and resurrection/second coming), realizing that within these boundaries is the present overlapping of the two ages. In other words, the believer must analyze and critique all non-Christian phenomena as one who is in the world but not of the world, as one who lives in the "present evil age" but belongs to and already has citizenship in heaven (II Corinth. 10:3-5; Phil. 3:20). There is not any structural discontinuity between the redemptive-historical period in which Paul lived and the redemptive-historical period in which the Christian now lives. True, the cultural surroundings of our day differ from the cultural surroundings of Paul's day. But although the cultural surroundings differ, nevertheless, all thought must be analyzed within the constant boundaries of present eschatological history. If one avoids this eschatological contruction, it is probable that one's apologetic approach will be dictated by one's cultural situation rather than by the sovereignty of God. If one's cultural situation dictates one's apologetic approach, it is more than likely that Christianity will plunge into a religion of synthesis. The history of the church bears this testimony of synthesis (e.g. in the early church, there was Platonism and Neoplatonism; in the medieval church, there was Neoplatonism and Aristotelianism; and in the modern church, there are many representations, but in the Reformed tradition Platonism, Aristotelianism, Cartesianism and Scottish common sense philosophy have their supporters). On the other hand, if we understand eschatology as the prolegomena to Christian apologetics, and the two-age construction as the necessary starting point of eschatological apologetics, we realize that any synthesis thinking ruins the absolute genuineness and sanctity of the Christian religion. Here we must stand.

The Christian apologist should realize, therefore, that the starting point of his religion must begin by presupposing the self-attesting God of the Scriptures. The traditional method of apologetics fails to accept this point. According to the traditional apologist, reason must be the starting point of apologetics because reason must judge, examine, and interpret all things as well as assent to our conclusions concerning those things.[36] In other words, reason appre-

---

[36] A few examples of this are St. Thomas Aquinas, On the Truth of the Catholic Faith: God; trans. Anton C. Pegis I (Garden City: Image Books, 1955), pp. 59-97; John Locke, The Reasonableness of Christianity, ed. I. T. Ramsey (Stanford: Stanford University Press, 1958), pp. 2-77; Francis R. Beattie, Apologetics: or the Rational Vindication of Christianity (Richmond: Presby-

hends the truth. This conception of reason is said to be both "natural" and "neutral." It is said to be natural because it functions in the same manner for all men. It is said to be neutral because the traditional apologist claims that he is only describing the universal function of reason without holding any preconceived ideas about the concept of reason. This understanding of reason, however, is misleading. Reason is always defined from an individual perspective; it cannot be said to be neutral. The traditional method has placed reason within such a perspective. It has defined reason within a perspective determined by Greek philosophical thought, especially as it is found in Plato and Aristotle. Modern philosophical thought can only contribute to this definition as long as it remains consistent with a Greek conception of reason or as long as it is a logical extension of it. The traditional approach, therefore, sacrifices reason upon the altar of autonomous philosophical thought. For this approach, at the beginning of the apologetic task, reason operates outside the realm of a universe defined in Christian terms. Is this a consistent understanding of reason for Christianity? I think not. The rational faculty of man exists only because the God of the Bible created it. A Christian apologist should not, therefore, initiate this apologetic project by assuming nothing but the rational faculty of man, which is defined by the creature (as in Greek philosophy) instead of the Creator. By defining reason within the framework of Greek philosophy, the traditional apologist returns to a state of existence under the old creation, that is, he begins his defense upon speculative reason, disregarding the fact that Christ claims every step of the apologetic procedure. Thus, traditional apologetics fail because it accepts sin-darkened, mortal reason as its starting point. This conception of reason has already fallen under the final judgment of God. If the traditional method continues to thrive, the church will continue to surrender ground to the subtle forms of human autonomy which are implicit in the traditional apologetic approach.

terian Committee of Publication, 1903). It is interesting that on pages 19-32 of this work an introduction is written by Benjamin B. Warfield endorsing its contents. Warfield's introduction also appears in the volume entitled <u>Selected Shorter Writings of Benjamin B. Warfield</u>, ed. John E. Meeter II (Nutley: Presbyterian and Reformed Publishing Company, 1973), pp. 93-105.

We have not, therefore, completely identified the Christian's apologetic task until we relate the Christian to the corporate body of Christ, the church. We have focused upon the death and resurrection of Christ and its meaning for the structure and arrangement of theology. We have shown how this approach opposes a rational-individualistic method of theology and therefore also has shunned any rationalistic method of apologetics. Even within our approach, however, there is the danger of stressing the individual in our theological procedure. The final step which prevents this from occurring is an understanding of the relationship between the individual and the corporate body of Christ. We shall investigate this relationship in the context of the apologetic task.

An eschatological apologetic is also an ecclesiastical apologetic. One's apologetic must always occur within the context of the death and resurrection of Christ and Christ's establishment of His church (Mt. 16:18). Paul sees his own life in this manner. Paul speaks of himself as one who persecuted the church (I Cor. 15:10, 11; Gal. 1:13), but after the risen Christ appeared to him on the road to Damascus, as one who faithfully defends the church (I Cor. 15:10, 11; Gal. 1:22, 23; Col. 1:24, 25). When addressing the churches, Paul views believers as members of the corporate body of Christ's church. They are called saints (Rom. 1:6, 7; I Cor. 1:2; II Cor. 1:1; Eph. 1:1; Phil. 1:1; Col. 1:3) or brethren (Gal. 1:11; I Thess. 1:4; II Thess. 1:3) who have been separated unto the gospel of Christ. Even when Paul writes to Timothy, Titus, and Philemon, the corporate church is of primary importance in his addresses (cf. I Tim. 1:3-7; II Tim. 4:1-5; Titus 1:5-9; Philemon 10). Paul reminds the church that in defending it we are defending the promise of Christ (Mt. 16:18), which is being effected by the Holy Spirit's guidance of the church (Rom. 8:31-39; II Cor. 4:4-6; Eph. 3:10).[37]

I think it is evident in the writings of Paul

[37] A statement by Lucien Cerfaux in his work *The Christian in the Theology of St. Paul* (New York: Herder and Herder, 1967), p. 165, is appropriate here: "The eschatological struggle is being waged unceasingly during every moment of the Christian age. The cross, the resurrection and the founding of his church made Christ's victory manifest. We share in his triumph, but we also share in a war which will go on until the hostile powers are wiped out."

that the believer must defend the message of the church, not his personal religious experience or intellectual comprehension of the gospel. This ecclesiastical defense is expressed when the apologist makes his call to repentance and faith on the part of the unbeliever. It is not a call performed in abstraction to an isolated individual, rather it is a call to the unbeliever to find the meaning of his existence in the covenant body of Christ--the church. The traditional method of apologetics breaks down at this point. It does not understand the position of the individual within the corporate body of Christ; nor does it comprehend that the church is a direct outgrowth of the establishment of the kingdom of God in history (Mt. 16:19).[38] As a result, the traditional method places ecclesiology before eschatology in the encyclopedia of theology. This establishes an individualistic approach to the doctrine of the church,[39] which is one good reason why para-ecclesiastical organizations more readily accept the traditional apologetic method as their own. The works of Josh McDowell, Francis A. Schaeffer, Paul E. Little, and R. C. Sproul provide these organizations with an individualistic approach to apologetics which does not place much emphasis upon the organizational stance of ecclesiology.[40]

Different from this, my apologetic method discusses the topic of ecclesiology under the heading of theology as eschatology. Ecclesiology appears in the context of eschatology,[41] and therefore also

[38] cf. Geerhardus Vos, *The Teaching of Jesus Concerning the Kingdom of God and the Church* (Nutley: Presbyterian and Reformed Publishing Company, 1972), p. 12.

[39] In the Pauline doctrine of the church there is a unity (corporate body of believers) and plurality (individual members of the body). There is, however, *a priori* of the former with respect to viewing ecclesiology. This fact was brought out clearly in chapter 3 concerning the situation in the Corinthian church.

[40] cf. Josh McDowell, *Evidence That Demands a Verdict: Historical Evidences for the Christian Faith* (n. p.: Campus Crusade for Christ, Inc., 1972); Francis A. Schaeffer, *The God Who Is There* (Downers Grove: Inter-Varsity Press, 1968); Paul E. Little, *Know Why You Believe* (Wheaton: Victor Books [14th printing], 1977); and R. C. Sproul, *The Psychology of Atheism* (Minneapolis: Bethany Fellowship, Inc., 1974).

[41] This is why Vos can say that the church should be defined the following way: "the church is that new congregation taking the place of the old congregation of Israel, which is formed by Jesus as the Messiah and stands under his Messianic rule" (*The Teaching of Jesus Concerning the Kingdom of God and the*

precedes apologetics. We can only conclude from this that a truly Christian apologetic is an apologetic of the church.

The significance of the two-age construction for Christian eschatological apologetics is that it defines the antithetical starting point from which the whole discipline of apologetics follows; it does not provide a whole apologetic system. The two-age construction clearly defines the eschatological stance of the apologist, and at the same time it defines his opponent. The importance of this is obvious: an apologist not only has to know what to defend from the outset, but in performing his task, he must also know against whom he is constructing a defense. Probably more than any other passage in Paul, I Corinthians 1-3 provides the apologist with a precise definition of the two sides.[42] As we stated, Paul's concern was that the Corinthians define their lives in terms of eschatological Christocentric existence. At every point, our Christian faith (this includes all our disciplines, even apologetics) must always be focused upon the truth of what God has done in Christ. I Corinthians 1-3 instructs us where apologetics must begin: with the absolute antithetical nature of the eschatological two-ages, the "Wisdom of God" versus the "wisdom of men," the kingdom of God versus the kingdom of Satan. To begin at any other point would

Church, p. 79).

[42]This history of interpretation has definitely demonstrated the relevance of apologetics in I Corinthians 1-3. Philip Edgcumbe Hughes for example, speaks in his article, "Crucial Biblical Passages for Christian Apologetics," p. 138, about I Corinthians 2:14. Conzelmann, An Outline of the Theology of the New Testament, p. 244ff, discusses the apologetic question of the "possibility of a natural knowledge of God" from I Corinthians 1:18ff. The apologetic question concerning the relationship between faith and reason has also appeared in the context of I Corinthians 1-3. An example of this is H. L. Goudge, The First Epistle to the Corinthians (London: Methuen and Company, 1903), p. 11. I Corinthians 1-3 has also been analyzed as a parallel to Romans 1:18ff with regard to apologetic issues (cf. Hodge, An Exposition of the First Epistle to the Corinthians, p. 21; Conzelmann, An Outline of the Theology of the New Testament, p. 244; William Childs Robinson, Jr., "Word and Power (I Corinthians 1:17-2:5)," Soli Deo Gloria: New Testament Studies in Honor of William Childs Robinson, ed. J. McDowell Richards (Richmond: John Knox Press, 1968), p. 69. This is a small sample of the huge amount of material on these apologetic subjects as they appear in I Corinthians 1-3.

negate the uniqueness of the Christian message.

Any apologetic system which does not begin, therefore, with the eschatological structure of Paul's thought, is carnal apologetics. In order to make this statement we must realize that the "jealousy and strife" (3:2) which arose in the Corinthian church was an expression of their failure to grasp the uniqueness of eschatological existence. The ability to grasp eschatological existence does not mean that an eschatological apologetic is more important than a carnal apologetic. Rather, the eschatological apologetic reflects more completely the "perfect" or "mature" life of the church (2:6) as well as the "spiritual" nature of the church (2:10-16) as it confronts the "world of the flesh." One can never adequately confront the "world of the flesh" by synthesizing apologetics with the ways of the flesh (3:3). The issue is whether the church is going to accept an apologetic which is religiously mature (eschatological apologetic) or an apologetic which is religiously immature (carnal apologetic). My hope is that the church will establish itself with Paul in the <u>eschaton</u>.

Since the two-age construction is the starting point of Christian apologetics, we must now define the two ages for the apologetic task. The direction of this task has been implied in Chapters 2 and 3 of this work. It would be good for us to condense this material and apply it to apologetics. However, as I stated, we are defending the "age to come" as an all-inclusive or holistic system of truth against the "present evil age" as an all-inclusive or holistic system of falsity. The two-age construction defines the all-inclusive response of man to the revelation of God. God reveals to Paul that He views the heart and existence of man in relationship to whatever aeon man may belong. This means that from the beginning of our apologetic, we must submit to the way God views man in his eschatological condition. Man is of Christ or of Satan. There is no neutral ground; all systems of thought either flow from Christ or from Satan.[43]

[43]This is one subject in which the writings of Van Til make a solid contribution. Van Til will never compromise the gospel of Jesus Christ for the sake of neutrality. The traditional apologist uses reason, for the sake of reaching the individual, as a neutral area in which he can converse and proceed in discussion. Such a position surrenders a thorough Christian-theistic system of defending a biblical truth to the unbeliever.

If one claims neutrality, therefore, he aligns himself with Satan. On the other hand, if one synthesizes that which is of Christ with that which is of Satan, he is "carnal" or "fleshly" (as was the problem in Corinth). Neither one of these latter two positions is condoned by the kingdom of Christ. The point is this: one cannot serve two masters, Christ and the world (Satan). This is why the two-age construction occupies the starting point of our apologetic. From the initial stage of our apologetic system, it differentiates the Christian world and life view from the non-Christian world and life view. When the Christian apologist, therefore, analyzes and critiques various non-Christian systems of thought (e.g. Platonism, Aristotelianism, Hegelianism, and many others), it should become obvious that those systems lack a Biblical world and life view. The two-age construction is a marvelous asset in maintaining the sanctity and uniqueness of the Christian message. This is at the heart of Paul's message.

When applying the two-age construction to apologetics, the Christian apologist is reminded of the fact that he is a member of the "age to come" and as such defends the all-inclusive concepts of that aeon. His apologetic task is to defend the "wisdom of God." He must defend the eternal sovereign plan of God the Father, who hid His wisdom in a mystery until He revealed the mystery of divine Wisdom in the power and work of His Son, Jesus Christ. Jesus Christ, the Wisdom of God, has now been revealed. Our apologetic must begin with Jesus Christ and His message of redemption and it must end with Jesus Christ and His message of redemption. An eschatological apologetic is a messianic apologetic. It is the full-orbed eschatological message of the gospel (word of the cross). This does not mean that a messianic apologetic is limited to the specific time when Christ initially appeared on the face of the earth to the time when He shall come again (parousia). As we have hinted previously, the full-orbed eschatological message of Christ also includes the concept that "by Him [Christ] all things were created, in the heavens and on earth, visible and invisible, whether thrones or dominions or rulers or authorities. All things have been created by Him and for Him. And He is before all things and in Him all things hold together" (Col. 1:16, 17). The historical death and resurrection of Christ is the focal point of Christ's meaning for the creation, since the creation was made by and for Him. A messianic apologetic defends Christ as the meaning of the creation from creation's beginning through its consummation, which has now been fulfilled and revealed to His covenant people in the "age to come." The apologist affirms that Jesus Christ alone has lasting importance for the salvation of man.

Since it is a messianic apologetic, it is also a heavenly apologetic by virtue of the work of the Holy Spirit in the Messiah's church. The Holy Spirit is now the permanent possession of Christ's new covenant people in the "age to come." For this reason, the apologist must understand that it is the Holy Spirit who demonstrates and authenticates the truth of the gospel which he is proclaiming to the unbelieving evil aeon. The Holy Spirit enables our apologetic to confront powerfully the "present evil age" by remaining fortified with the spiritual existence of heaven. If any member, therefore, of the "present evil age" is transformed into the "age to come" it must be understood as solely accomplished by the Holy Spirit. Our apologetic task and its accomplishment rests solely upon the sovereign gracious work of God; it does not rely upon man's systems to attract people into the kingdom of God.[44] Our apologetic must submit to the fact that all things are working according to God's sovereign will. The apologist may be persecuted by the "present evil age" as Paul was at Lystra (Acts 14:19). At the same time, the apologist may find many disciples as the result of the proclamation of the gospel (Acts 14:21). There is no doubt that the apologetic task is difficult, for the apologist realizes he is living in the present tension or drama between the "age to come" and the "present evil age." Nevertheless, by belonging to the "age to come," he has the assurance of victory over the kingdom of Satan. The church must comprehend that the power and strength of the victorious Christ and His Spirit are part of the church's construction. The apologist of the church marches in this confidence, realizing that such an

---

[44]Commenting on I Corinthians 2:7, I find Alan Richardson's statement in his *An Introduction to the Theology of the New Testament*, p. 58, both interesting and appropriate for apologetics at this point: "The mysterious truth of the Gospel cannot be made known through ordinary publicity channels but only through 'the hearing of faith' -- a truth constantly overlooked by busy, untheological clergymen who imagine that they can bring home the message of the Gospel by modern advertising techniques and business methods. Thus they convert the mystery of evangelization into a 'problem of communication.'"

apologetic carries with it the everlasting character of heaven itself.

The apologist of victory defends the "age to come" against the "present evil age" which defines man in union with Adam's fall into sin. He defends the historical aeon of the Last Adam, the Wisdom of God," against the rebelling historical aeon of the First Adam, the "wisdom of the world." The First Adam's wisdom responds to the revelation of God by demanding God to further authenticate Himself by the criteria of the world's wisdom. It is a wisdom which has its origin in man, and it defies the wisdom which has its origin in God. The revelation of God always fails such human criteria for absolute truth because the "present evil age" sets itself up as the authority and judge of God's truth, and it judges God's revelation as foolishness.[45] The wisdom of the world finds its truth in a lie instead of in what is actually true. The "present evil age" is anti-Christocentric, anti-Spiritual, anti-soteriological, and anti-theocentric Kingdom. At the same time it endorses that which is worldly (kosmos), fleshly, autonomous, and of the kingdom of Satan. The greatest example of worldly wisdom is that the world's rulers condemned the Son of God to death.

The Christian apologist understands that God has never endorsed such a wisdom, but has condemned it (I Cor. 1:18). The Christian apologist also understands that the discipline of apologetics exists only because the "present evil age" exists. We cannot overemphasize this point. This verifies the fact that any synthesis with the "present evil age" loses the distinctiveness of the eternal Christian message; it loses the purpose of apologetics. The eschatological dimension, therefore, which determines the Christian's apologetic task is set against the "present evil age," realizing that: 1) the apologist continues to live in the kosmos, 2) the apologist is not of the kosmos, and 3) the apologist is sent to proclaim and defend Christ's message of heavenly existence to the kosmos.[46]

[45]As Conzelmann, A Commentary on the First Epistle to the Corinthians, p. 55, writes: "God's wisdom is defined in I Corinthians 1:24 as 'Christ', as a wisdom which does not subject itself to human criteria, but confounds all such criteria."

[46]These three points are suggested by Bromiley, "World," p. 967.

I return to the content of Chapter 1 as it now applies to what I have been saying in this chapter. At the end of the section on Plato, I raised the following questions: How is Paul's two-age construction antithetical to Plato's view? How does Paul's formulation provide the Christian with a defense against Plato? Starting with the first question we address ourselves immediately to Paul and Plato's antithetical constructions. We begin by noting that Paul's two-age construction is antithetical to Plato's formulation of the two world orders because Plato does not begin with the biblical conception of God, nor does his whole system present a biblical world and life view. The origin of Paul's construction is the distinct, infallible revelation of God, whereas the origin of Plato's thought is Greek philosophical tradition and his own speculative thought. In other words, the origin of Plato's thought is in human wisdom or in human observation of the so-called "rational order of things." Plato constructs the Ideal world and the world of matter with his rational mind. With respect to God, Plato's Demiurge (God) is a mythical independent mediator (standing for something real --divine Reason). The Demiurge brings chaotic matter into a high degree of perfection (Becoming), using the Ideal world as a model or blueprint (Being). In this construction God (Demiurge) does not occupy the supreme level. Instead he is a mediator between two world orders. According to Paul, God cannot hold such a position. God is absolutely supreme; He does not submit to any being, concept, principle, or world order. He is not a mediator between Becoming and Being.

With regard to the world and life view, Plato's formulation of two world orders conditions him as Paul's formulation of the two-ages conditions him. Plato's two world orders are a dualistic mythical conception of Being. The one is the real and unchangeable object of belief or opinion (Ideal world), whereas the other is connected with the irrational or inexpressible sensation of a thing (Matter). The distinction between Plato's two worlds is ontological. On the other hand, Paul's two-ages are anchored in the sovereign work of God in history. The "present evil age" is under the judgment of God because of man's sin whereas the "age to come" is the redemption of God in Jesus Christ for His people. Two entities exist within history, but this is not a dualistic cosmology; Paul's distinction between the two ages is not ontological but historical and ethical as well as religious.[47]

Since Plato's cosmological dualism is ontological, he views the <u>kosmos</u> (world of Matter) as ethically good, since the Demiurge rationally ordered the <u>kosmos</u> good after the Form of Absolute Good. Plato's God is, therefore, teleological: the Demiurge, who is imminent in its relationship with the <u>kosmos</u>, formed the <u>kosmos</u> so that it would orient <u>itself</u> towards the Good. From this perspective, Plato cannot penetrate the historical and ethical character of the creation. There is no place in the structure of his thought for the Christian view of the Fall as it has affected man in history. On the other hand, Paul understands the <u>kosmos</u> as evil. The word "<u>kosmos</u>" is so much associated with evil in Paul's writings that one cannot find the term used in reference to the new heaven and earth. In all of this, one can clearly observe that Paul's two-age construction is antithetical to Plato's formulation of two existing world orders. My purpose has been to show, using Plato as an example, that Christianity has no basis for effecting a synthesis with any non-Christian system of thought. One cannot synthesize Christianity with a non-Christian system and expect to produce a distinct Christian position. All non-Christian systems of thought reduce man to a creature of the "present evil age," whereas the Christian position expands and transforms man into the restored image of Christ and thus places redeemed man in the fulness of the "age to come."

Correct epistemology is also vital to Christian apologetics. The construction of a Christian epistemology must always include in its foundation the true interpretation of revelation as well as the consideration of the ethical condition of man. This point

---

[47]Though I do not care for Ladd's phrase "biblical dualism," I am in basic agreement with his point when he writes that "biblical dualism is utterly different from this Greek view. It is religious and ethical, not cosmological. The world is God's world; man is God's creature, although rebellious, sinful and fallen. Salvation is achieved not by a flight from the world to God; it means, in effect, God's descent from heaven to bring man in historical experience into fellowship with himself. Therefore the consummation of salvation is eschatological" (<u>The Pattern of New Testament Truth</u>, p. 14). This quotation appears in the context of Ladd's rejection of the idea that the New Testament, especially Paul's theology, is influenced by Gnostic elements of which Platonic dualism is the basic source.

is extremely important because any failure to perceive it leads to the construction of a synthetic apologetic system. The traditional method of apologetics, for example, approaches epistemology with reason as the starting point. The traditional apologist maintains that there is a universal theory of knowledge based on natural and neutral reason since the faculty of reason has remained intact after the fall of man into sin. In his estimation, reason still perceives, examines, judges, and interprets correctly. The traditional apologist appeals to the common knowledge of creation that he and the unbeliever share through the faculty of reason. Using this common knowledge as a foundation, the apologist will present an argument for the reasonableness of Christianity. The traditional method holds that the reasonableness of Christianity can be clearly <u>demonstrated</u> to the unbeliever. It holds, however, that the unbeliever cannot be <u>persuaded</u> of the reasonableness and truthfulness of Christianity except by the power of the Holy Spirit. This gulf between the demonstration of Christianity to the unbeliever and the persuasion of the unbeliever to Christianity exists because of sin. Sin prevents the unbeliever from being persuaded of that which is reasonable to believe. Only the power and conviction of the Holy Spirit can bring the unbeliever to a true knowledge of Jesus Christ and to an accurate understanding of God's creation. Thus, the traditional method states that epistemology has its final certainty in an intimate relationship with the Creator. Here, knowledge is <u>really true</u>.

Such a dualistic conception of epistemology (based upon reason as well as the Holy Spirit) receives no endorsement from the Apostle Paul because Paul does not view man in abstraction from his ethical condition before God. In Romans 1:18-32, for example, this is clearly evident. In this text Paul affirms the justice of God's wrath against all those who live in ungodliness and unrighteousness (vs. 18). The wrath of God is righteous because all unbelief has unrighteously suppressed the true interpretation of God's creation and walked thanklessly before God (vs. 18, 21). Thus, the unbeliever has "exchanged the truth of God for a lie, and worshiped and served the creature rather than the Creator" (vs. 25). In other words, Romans 1:18-32 describes members of the "present evil age," as subjects of sin and Satan. It is a description of man rejecting his Creator with his entire being. Paul's concern is not to present the extent of man's natural knowledge of God; nor is his concern to acknowledge an agreement between himself and the Greek philosophers in constructing a rational and natural knowledge of the deity. As a matter of fact, judging from Paul's words, it can be said that the Greek philosophers (including Plato) fall within the scope of God's wrath, since they never worshiped the Creator, but instead worshiped the creature. It should be emphasized, therefore, that this passage contains no dualistic conception of epistemology. According to Paul, man stands either in the knowledge of the "present evil age" -- in unrighteousness before God's wrath, or man stands in the knowledge of the "age to come" -- in God's righteousness to everyone who believes (vs. 16, 17).

A biblical theory of epistemology states, therefore, that one's own epistemological stance is conditioned by the age to which one belongs. If one's theory of epistemology is to be Christian, then, one should submit his knowledge to the revelation of God in the eschatological age to come. The Holy Spirit convicts and persuades the believer and interprets the facts correctly in God's created universe for the believer in Christ. The unbeliever, who is dominated by the present evil age, is neither convicted nor persuaded; nor does he interpret the facts correctly, since he refuses to believe that all things have been created through Christ and unto Christ (Col. 1:16).[48] Jesus Christ must be at the heart of the believer's knowledge of revelation, because from Christ, through Christ and unto Christ are all things (Rom. 11:36.) The unbeliever has no idea of this knowledge of reality.[49]

[48]As John Calvin comments on I Corinthians 1:20, "Let us, then, take notice, that we must restrict to the specialties of the case in hand that Paul here teaches, respecting the unity of the wisdom of this world -- that it rests in the mere elements of the world, and does not reach to heaven. In other respects, too, it holds true, that without Christ sciences in every department are vain, and that the man who knows not God is vain, though he should be conversant with every branch of learning" (Commentary on the Epistles of Paul the Apostle to the Corinthians, I. p. 83).

[49]For further discussion of epistemology in the context of the two-ages consult J. Louis Martyn's article "Epistemology at the Turn of the Ages: II Corinthians 5:16," in Christian History and Interpretation: Studies Presented to John Knox, ed. W. F. Farmer, C. F. D. Moule, and R. R. Niebuhr (Cambridge: At the University Press, 1964), pp. 409-421.

In a real sense, therefore, Paul's two-age construction provides the Christian with a defense against Plato. Let me highlight and summarize: the two-age construction is used by the Christian apologist to identify his opponent and define the antithetical structure of the two systems--Christianity and Platonism. The apologist defends the whole council of God as a member of the "age to come," while at the same time he analyzes and critiques Plato's system as one which belongs to the "present evil age." It belongs to the "present evil age" because Plato constructed a system which glorified human wisdom. Plato was guilty of molding and shaping the creation into his own autonomous dualistic system. Plato did not construct a revealed system, but a Satanic system. His system is identified and defined by the Christian use of the two ages, and thus a biblical apologetic task has begun against him.

Paul's two-age construction also provides the Christian with a defense against the view of eschatology found in Jewish apocalyptic literature. In chapter 1, I already provided the foundation for an apologetic analysis and critique of the eschatological position of Jewish apocalyptic literature. In light of what we have said in chapter 4, it would be well for us to clarify our analysis and critique. In chapter 1 we confronted basically two issues: 1) the popular issue that Paul's eschatology is a synthesis of the formulation of apocalyptic literature (Käsemann), and 2) whether or not the structure and substance of eschatology presented in the literature itself provided any warrant for a Pauline synthesis. At this time, I merely wish to underline my conclusion that Paul's eschatological framework is unique because it is a formulation received by divine revelation as it fits organically within the history of redemption. This is quite different from the structure and substance of eschatology presented in apocalyptic literature. As we have seen, it presents a Jewish, ethnic, Messianic Kingdom which is political, national, earthly, and provisional. According to the organic revelation of the history of redemption, Paul could never accept this position. (The Abrahamic covenant was never ethnic, it was universal -- Gen. 17:5, 6; Gal. 3:29; I Tim. 2:7). Käsemann is asking us to accept a selfish, ethnic, inconsistent eschatological framework as the "mother" of Paul's eschatological framework.[50] I believe that Käsemann's position is inconceivable. If he had actually understood Paul's two-age construction, he would have realized that Jewish apocalyptic eschatology, as a complete system, belongs to the "present evil age." It is based on man's wisdom and has forsaken the revealed wisdom of God. In light of this, Paul's two-age construction is, therefore, an apologetic defense against the false conception of apocalyptic eschatology. Using Jewish apocalyptic literature as an example, we must acknowledge that the substance and framework of Paul's eschatology proves itself to be a distinctive formulation. Paul does not synthesize a Jewish apocalyptic view of eschatology with a redemptive-historical view of eschatology.

If what I have been saying concerning Paul's theology as it applies to the discipline of apologetics is true, we are forced to conclude that the history of apologetics must be reevaluated in the light of eschatological apologetics. The task is set before us to have a clearly non-synthetic apologetic method and system; there is no synthesis between worldly thought and Christian eschatological thought. We must, therefore, rid ourselves of such historical apologetic syntheses as: early Christian apologists and Greek Logos idea, Augustine and neo-Platonism, Aquinas and Aristotelianism, Locke and rationalism, and Hodge and scientific rationalism. Although there are many syntheses, these are a few which have had a lasting influence upon Christian apologetics. The task before the evangelical and Reformed communities is not simple or easy. It will be a long and tedious task if we are to clear the slate of synthetic apologetics. Some would even argue that it is impossible. Although this may be true, we nevertheless are obligated to be thoroughly consistent to God's revelation. This must be our allegiance and our goal. It is imperative, therefore, that we establish ourselves in an

[50]As William Manson summarizes in "Eschatology in the New Testament," "It is impossible to think that traditional apocalyptic ideas are here made plastic to the needs of a genuinely higher religious experience [New Testament kerygma]. Rather, as the introduction into the picture of cosmology, astrology, angelology, and demonology shows, the development which takes place in apocalyptic thought is speculative and gnostic rather than religious in its inspiration. I intend, therefore, to leave this period to one side as not bearing very materially on the essence of the Christian eschatology..." (p. 2).

eschatological apologetic. It is the apolgetic of "resurrection," of an existence which is living, eternal, non-temporal and heavenly in Christ (characteristics of the "age to come"). It is not an apologetic of "death," of an existence which is dying, perishing, temporal and earthly (characteristcs of the "present evil age").

Let me now summarize the significance of the two-age construction for Christian eschatological apologetics, recalling first that we are to remain faithful to the sovereign work of God in history. With this in mind, the significance of the two-ages is as follows: 1) it helps to define the place of apologetics in the encyclopedia of theology, 2) it defines the task and starting point of apologetics within the concept of redemptive history, 3) it outlines the antithetical structure of Christianity from the beginning of the apologetic task until the consummation of that task, 4) it leads to a distinctive Christian apologetic because of its non-synthetic character, and 5) it provides the starting point of analysis and critique of non-Christian systems which fail to view man as the image of Christ.

SELECTED BIBLIOGRAPHY

Cornford, Francis MacDonald. *Plato's Cosmology: The 'Timaeus' of Plato Translated with a Running Commentary*. New York: Humanities Press, 1952.

Cross, R. C. and A. D. Woozley. "Knowledge, Belief, and the Forms," *Plato: A Collection of Critical Essays*, ed. Gregory Vlastos. Vol. I. Garden City: Doubleday, 1971. 70-96.

Ellis, Earle E. *Paul and His Recent Interpreters*. Grand Rapids: Wm. B. Eerdmans, 1961.

Gaffin, Richard B., Jr. "Systematic Theology and Biblical Theology," *The New Testament Student and Theology*, ed. John H. Skilton. Vol. III. n.p.: Presbyterian and Reformed, 1976.

_____. *The Centrality of the Resurrection: A Study in Paul's Soteriology*. Grand Rapids: Baker, 1978.

Geehan, E. R., ed. *Jerusalem and Athens: Critical Discussions on the Philosophy and Apologetics of Cornelius Van Til*. n.p.: Presbyterian and Reformed, 1971.

Grosheide, F. W. *Commentary on the First Epistle to the Corinthians*. Grand Rapids: Wm. B. Eerdmans, 1953.

Halsey, Jim S. *For a Time Such as This: An Introduction to the Reformed Apologetic of Cornelius Van Til*. n.p.: Presbyterian and Reformed, 1976.

Hamilton, Neill Q. *The Holy Spirit and Eschatology in Paul*. Edinburgh: Oliver & Boyd, 1957.

Hodge, Charles. *Systematic Theology*. 3 vols. New York: Charles Scribner's Sons, 1899.

Jeremias, Joachim. "The Key to Pauline Theology," *The Expository Times*, LXXVI (October, 1964-September, 1965), 27-30.

Käsemann, Ernst. *New Testament Questions of Today*, trans. W. J. Montague. London: SCM Press, 1969.

Ladd, George Eldon. *The Pattern of New Testament Truth*. Grand Rapids: Wm. B. Eerdmans, 1968.

Machen, J. Gresham. *The Origin of Paul's Religion*. Grand Rapids: Wm. B. Eerdmans, 1925.

Morris, Leon. *Apocalyptic*. Grand Rapids: Wm. B. Eerdmans, 1972.

Murray, John. *Redemption: Accomplished and Applied*. Grand Rapids: Eerdmans, 1955.

_____. "Systematic Theology," *The New Testament Student and Theology*. Vol. III. n. p.: Presbyterian and Reformed, 1976. 18-31.

Ridderbos, Herman. *Paul: An Outline of His Theology*, trans. John Richard De Witt. Grand Rapids: Wm. B. Eerdmans, 1975.

_____. *When the Time Had Fully Come: Studies in New Testament Theology*. Grand Rapids: Wm. B. Eerdmans, 1957.

Van Til, Cornelius. *An Introduction to Systematic Theology*. Philadelphia: Class Syllabus, 1970.

_____. *Apologetics*. Philadelphia: Class Syllabus, n. d.

_____. *The Defense of the Faith*. Philadelphia: Presbyterian and Reformed, 1967.

Vos, Geerhardus. "The Eschatological Aspect of the Pauline Conception of the Spirit," *Biblical and Theological Studies*. New York: Charles Scribner's Sons, 1912. 209-259.

_____. *The Pauline Eschatology*. Grand Rapids: Wm. B. Eerdmans, 1972.

INDEX OF SCRIPTURES

OLD TESTAMENT

Genesis
  3 p.34
  17:5,6 p.114

Exodus
  4:22 p.42
  23:19 p.43

Leviticus
  23:10 p.43

Numbers
  15:20f p.43
  18:8,11f,30 p.43

Deuteronomy
  18:4 p.43
  21:23 p.69
  26:1f p.43
  26:10 p.43

Psalms
  89:27 p.42
  94:11 p.73

Proverbs
  8:12-36 p.73
  8:17 p.73
  8:18-20 p.73
  8:30-34 p.73
  8:35 p.73

Isaiah
  11:2 p.74
  26:14 p.73
  28:6 p.74
  42:1 p.74
  59:21 p.74
  61:1 p.74

Jeremiah
  9:23-33 p.73

NEW TESTAMENT

Matthew
  12:39 p.70
  16:18 p.103
  16:19 p.104

Mark
  1:24 p.83
  1:34 p.83
  8:11 p.70

John
  2:18-22 p.71
  6:30 p.70

Acts
  3:17 p.83
  14:19 p.108
  14:21 p.108
  17 p.75
  17:22-31 p.75
  17:32-34 p.75
  17:32 p.76
  18:24 p.58
  18:25 p.58
  18:26 p.58

Romans
  1:6,7 p.103
  1:16,17 p.113
  1:18-32 p.112
  1:18ff p.105
  1:18 p.112
  1:21 p. 112
  1:25 p.112
  2:2 p.35
  3:6 p.36
  4:5 p.28
  5:1-5 p.28
  5:12-21 p.43,44
  5:12 p.44
  5:16 p.44
  5:17-19 p.44
  5:21 p.44
  6:5 p.47
  6:6,7 p.47
  6:9 p.47
  6:10 p.47
  6:11 p.47
  7:24,25 p.49
  8:1-4 p.28
  8:1 p.49,50
  8:2 p.46,49
  8:9 p.45,46,85

  8:10,11 p.46
  8:18ff p.48
  8:18 p.30
  8:28-30 p.28
  8:29 p.42
  8:31-39 p.103
  8:37-39 p.35
  11:15 p.30,37
  11:36 p.113
  12:1 p.48,56
  12:2 p.30,34,48
  16:25,26 p.28

I Corinthians
  1-3 p.38,105
  1:1-9 p.55
  1:2 p.56,57,63,108
  1:10-16 p.55
  1:10 p.55
  1:12 p.55,57,58,80
  1:17-2:6 p.64,69,72
  1:17-3:19 p.69
  1:17-3:23 p.72
  1:18-31 p.75
  1:18-2:5 p.65,69
  1:18-2:15 p.64
  1:18-3:20 p.55,105
  1:18 p.57,68,73,75-77,84,109
  1:19-2:16 p.66
  1:19 p.73
  1:20,21 p.36
  1:20 p.34,55,67,72,84,113
  1:21 p.67,77,84
  1:22 p.67,69
  1:23 p.67-69,72,76,84
  1:24 p.56,66-68,71-73,78,79,109
  1:26-30 p.79
  1:26 p.57,78
  1:27 p.78
  1:30 p.55-57,63,66,68,73-75,79,80
  1:31 p.73,78,81
  2:1 p.58,66,68,69,79

2:2 p.74
2:3 p.67,79
2:4 p.56,58,66,
68,69,79
2:5 p.56,57,66,
75,84
2:6-8 p.73,76,83
2:6-16 p.65,81
2:6 p.34,55,65-
67,80,84,108
2:7 p.28,55,65,
68,72,73,108
2:8 p.34,68,72,
73,82,83
2:9 p.73
2:10-13 p.76
2:10-16 p.106
2:10 p.57,74
2:11 p.68
2:12 p.36,68,80,
82,84
2:13 p.55,66,68,
75,80
2:14 p.67
2:15 p.80
2:16 p.73,80
3:1-3 p.55,82
3:1 p.64,80,82
3:2 p.76,106
3:3 p.80,85,106
3:6-9 p.80
3:6 p.58,61
3:9 p.85
3:11 p.85
3:16 p.57,80,85
3:17 p.80,85
3:18 p.34,66
3:19 p.66,68,73,
84
3:20 p.66,73
3:22 p.57,75,80
3:23 p.57,80
4:8 p.57
4:11 p.48
4:13 p.48,78
4:14,15 p.57
5:7 p.57
6:11 p.57
6:19 p.49,80
6:20 p.49
7:31 p.36

7:32-34 p.57
8:6 p.22,57
9:12 p.57
9:14 p.57
10:6 p.57
11:22 p.57
11:23 p.57
11:32 p.36
12:3 p.57
12:8 p.66
13:12 p.57
13:13 p.57
14:26 p.57
15:1-34 p.28
15:1 p.57
15:2 p.57
15:3,4 p.76
15:10 p.103
15:11 p.103
15:20ff p.43
15:21,22 p.44
15:22 p.41
15:42-49 p.43
15:42,43 p.44
15:45 p.44,45
15:45-47 p.44
15:49 p.44
15:49-53 p.45
16:12 p.61
16:13 p.57

II Corinthians
1:1 p.103
4:4-6 p.103
4:4 p.34,84
4:6 p.41
5:17 p.30,33,38,
41
5:19 p.37
6:2 p.30,33,41
7:10 p.36
10:3-5 p.101
11:22 p.57,61

Galatians
1:4 p.34,35
1:11-17 p.27
1:11 p.103
1:13 p.103
1:22 p.103
1:23 p.103
2:3 p.74

3:13 p.38
3:29 p.114
4:4 p.30,33
5:16-24 p.41
5:16ff p.48
5:17 p.46
5:19-21 p.46
5:22-26 p.46
6:4 p.38
6:14 p.78
6:15 p.38,47

Ephesians
1:1 p.103
1:4 p.78
1:9,10 p.28
1:10 p.74
1:14 p.45
1:20 p.47
1:21 p.35,39,45,47
2:2 p.35,46
2:6 p.47
2:7 p.39,45
2:12 p.45
3:3-5 p.28
3:10 p.103
4:4 p.45
4:13 p.82
4:30 p.45
5:6 p.45
6:12 p.48

Philippians
1:1 p.103
1:6 p.45
2:15 p.36
2:16 p.45
3:19 p.48
3:20 p.45,48,49,101

Colossians
1:3 p.103
1:15-20 p.28
1:15 p.41
1:16 p.22,113
1:16,17 p.107
1:18 p.41
1:24 p.103
1:25 p.103
1:26 p.28
2:2,3 p.28,82
2:20 p.43

3:1-17 p.43
3:1-4 p.28,42,47
3:1 p.42
3:2 p.48
3:3 p.47
3:4 p.41,45
6:24 p.45

I Thessalonians
1:4 p.78,103

II Thessalonians
1:3 p.103
2:10-12 p.49
2:13,14 p.49
2:15 p.49

I Timothy
1:3-7 p.103
1:15 p.38
2:7 p.114
6:17 p.34

II Timothy
1:9,10 p.28
1:10 p.42
4:1-5 p.103
4:10 p.34,35

Titus
1:2,3 p.28
1:5-9 p.103
2:12 p.34

Philemon
10 p.103

Revelation
1:8 p.97
1:17,18 p.76

49.2 p.21
49.4 p.20
51.1ff p.21
52.4 p.21
53.1ff p.21
54.1ff p.21
61.4 p.21
61.5,8 p.21
61.8ff p.20

II Enoch
65.7-10 p.24

Assumption of Moses
10.1 p.21
10.2 p.21
10.3-4 p.21
10.7 p.21
10.9-10 p.21

The Psalms of Solomon
17.23 p.19
17.24-27 p.19
17.28-30 p.19
17.30-32 p.19
17.31 p.19
17.34-36 p.19
17.39 p.19

INDEX OF APOCRYPHA AND PSEUDEPIGRAPHA

II Esdras
4:26 p.24

I Enoch
37-71 p.20
38.3 p.21
41.2 p.21
45.3 p.20
45.4-5 p.21
45.4 p.21
45.6 p.21
48.2f p.20

INDEX OF PERSONS AND SUBJECTS

Ackermann, C. 2
Adam 36,40,44
   first and last Adam 40,43,
   45,52,109
   last Adam 41,45
   first Adam 43-45
aeon 32-34,36,44-46,48-51,73,
106-108
   as eschatological 46
   as future 37,38,49
   as new (age) 34,36,39-41,
   44,46-48,50,52
   as old (evil age) 34,47,48,
   52,108
age to come cf. two-age construction
aion 34-36
Alexandria 59,61
analogical (knowledge of God)
91,94
analytical (knowledge of God) 91
Anthropology 87,89,116
antithesis 51,52,65,68,72,73,
77,80,85,100,105,110,111,116
Apollos 58-61
apologetics 65,75,98-106,108,
109,111,114-116
   as antithetical 100,105,109,
   114,116
   as carnal 106,107
   demonstration 99,105,106,112
   and ecclesiology 103-105,108
   as eschatological 100,101,
   104,106,109,111,115,116
   as heavenly 108,109,116
   holistic system 100,106
   as loci 98,116
   as messianic 107,108,116
   starting point 89,99-102,105-
   107,112,116
   as synthesis 101,106,107,109,
   111,112,116
   traditional method 99,101-
   104,106,112
   two-age construction 99-101,
   105,106,109
Apostles 78
Aquinas, Thomas 101,115
Areopagus 75,76

Aristotle 102
   Aristotelianism 101,107,
   115
   Aristotelian logic 88
Arminianism 90
Athens 75,76
atonement 95

Bammel, E. 57
Bandstra, A.J. 36,40
Barclay, W. 70,75
Barrett, C.K. 18,49,50,63,66-
68
Bauckham, R.J. 13,18,23,24
Baur, F.C. 57
Beardslee, J.W. 88
Beattie, F. 101
believer
   as chosen 78-79
   as citizens of two worlds
   48-51
   and corporate church 103
   crucifixion of 47,98
   election 78-79
   eternal life 75-76,116
   glorification of 85
   in Christ 78,81,95,106,113,
   116
   identity of 100
   in heaven 48,101
   in Spirit 80,85
   present state of 50,96,99
   resurrection of 47,87,98,
   116
   as saints 103
   sits in the heavenly places
   47,109
   union with Christ 42,43,46,
   47,49,85,97,98,100
   wisdom of 71
Berkhof, L. 87,90
Biblical theology 92-96,98
Bornkamm, G. 29,55,60,67,76,
84
Bromiley, G. 36,37,109
Brown, R.B. 84
Bruce, F.F. 63
Brunner, E. 32
Bultmann, R. 18,28-30,32,36,

Butler, Bishop J. 99
Caird, G.B. 83
Calvin, J. 56,70,74,79,85,113
Cambridge Platonists 2
Cassirer, E. 2
Catholocism 90
Celsus 70
Cephas 60
Charles, R.G. 17,18,19
Cherniss, H. 2,5,6
Christ (Jesus)
   as Alpha & Omega 97,107,108
   Christocentric 33,34,46,47,
   82,97,105
   Christology 29,47,65,87,96
   as Creator 107
   cross 66,69-71,75-78,80,81,
   103
   crucifixion 38,41,66,67,69-
   72,74-77,82-84
   death & resurrection 28,32,
   34,35,39,40,45-47,52,55,64,
   71,73,76,77,96,98,103,107
   eschatological work 28,41,
   44,46,47,50,74,95,98,100,107
   as eternal life 75,76
   as firstborn 40-43,45,52
   as firstfruits 41,43,45,52
   God-man 70
   as image of God 40,111,116
   as judge 73
   Kingship (Lordship) 51,76,
   77
   as Last Adam 43,44,109
   mystery of redemption 27,40,
   68,72-74,76,82,107
   resurrection 41,44,48,53,76,
   95,100,103
   as revelation 64,67,72,73,
   97,107
   rules (exalted) 35,40,41,
   46,73,75,104
   second coming 39,45,51,53,
   96,100,107,109
   as Son of God 40,41,71,107
   suffering 70,71,75
   as wisdom 72-74,76,82,85,
   100,105,107,109
Christian synthesis 1,2,9,12,
13,101
church 32,46,63,55,56,75,77,
78,80,82,96,102-106,108
citizenship 41,47-51,101
Clark, G. 6-8
cogito ergo sum 88
condemnation 45,50,84,85
Conzelmann, H. 62,63,71,76-78,
80,81,83,105,109
Copleston, F. 6,10
Corinthian church 55,56,104-107
   problem of 56,80,105-107
   factions of (parties) 57-62,
   64,74,80
   spiritual problem of 80-85,
   106,107
Cornford, F.M. 3-8,10,11
covenant 33,74,89,93,104,108
creation 35,39,42,74-76,107,108,
111-113
   as old creation 47,102
   as new creation 30,33,37-39,
   41,46,55
Creator-creature 90,92,102,112,
113
Cross, R.C. 4-6
Cullmann, O. 28,50,51,83

Dahl, N. 63
Descartes 88
   Cartesian logic 88
   Cartesianism 101
demons 83
demonstration (proof) 79,99,105,
106,112
dialectic 51
disciples 72,108
Dodd, C.H. 77
Dods, M. 75
Dooyeweerd, H. 1,96
dualism 46,59,111-114
DuPlessis, P.J. 81
Dupont, J. 57

Ebeling, G. 14
Ecclesiology 87,89,96,103,104
   para-ecclesiastical 104
Ellis, E.E. 63
Epicurean 88
epistemology 90,112,113
   as Christian 89,111-113
Eschatology 14,50,63,64,73,78,
80,87-89,95-97,100,101,103-106,

109,113,115
   already and not yet 31-33,41,
    47,50,51,81,100
   as antithesis 51,64,72,77,85
   as apocalyptic 14,15,18,20,
    25,32,114
   community 55,67
   <u>eschaton</u> 87,96,106
   history 99,101
   judgment 38
   last days (things) 28,40,88
   living 62-64,72,80,97,100,
    106,116
   as loci 90
   message of 64,72,75,76,78,
    79,82,84,100,105-107,109
   Paul's 14,16,25,28-33,38,41,
    46,47,64,72,74,77,80,106
   realized 62,96
   as system 99
   tension (struggling) 31-33,
    47,48,50,51,55,64,80,82,103,108
evangelical-Reformed 87,89
Evans, E. 58
Ewert, D. 49
exaltation 45
Existentialism 45,52
   Bultmann's view of 28,29,30,
    51,77
   existential 63
   existential interpretation of
    history 51

faith 47,50,52,53,74,78,79,88,
  97
   faith & repentance 104
   faith & reason 105
Fall into sin 34-37,44,46,72,
  84,111,112
Ferch, A.J. 22
Ficino, M. 2
Filson, F. 50
Fisher, G. 99
Fjarstedt, B. 67
flesh 34,48
   fleshly 82,107,109
   flesh & spirit 40,45,59
   man of flesh 64
   way of the flesh 41,46,52,
    83,100,106
   world of flesh 47-49,85

Flint, R. 99
foolishness 66,68,70,76-78,84,
  100,109
Foster, M.B. 11
Frost, S.B. 17,19
Fuchs, E. 60
fulness of time 30,33,40,41,43,
  52,53,99,100,111
Funk, R. 55,79

Gaffin, R.B. 42,43,50,95,96,98
Gager, J.G. 32
Gartner, B. 73,81
Gassendi, P. 88
Gentiles 64,67
Gerstner, J.G. 99
glorification 45,85,95
Gnostics 60,64,68,111,115
   gnosticism 61,62,65
   as Jewish Christian 59
   as mythological 59,61,68,69
God 10,11,16,18,23,24,28,33,
  36,38,50,69,89,110
   as Father 42,68,74,76,77
   Godhead 68,89,94,99
   grace of 38,46,78,100,108
   judgments of 36,37,44,72,73,
    84,87,102,110
   knowledge of 84,91,92,112,
    113
   providence of 33,52
   as self-attesting 89,101
   as sovereign 30,78,89,90,94,
    97-101,107,108,110,116
   rationality of 90-92
Goudge, H.L. 105
Gould, J. 11,12
Greek (s) 69-72,76,78,111,115
Greek philosophy 1,45,64,69-71,
  102,110,113
Grosheide, F.W. 57,60,79,83,85
Guthrie, D. 62

Hackett, S. 99
Hackforth, R. 8,10,11
Halsey, J.S. 91
Hamilton, F. 99
Hamilton, N.Q. 30,46
Hanson, P.D. 18
Hare, R.M. 4
Härrison, R.K. 17

heaven 79,85,108,109,111,113
   heavenly places 47
   citizen of heaven 47-49,80, 101
Hegelian philosophy 57
   Hegelianism 107
<u>Heilsgut</u> 66,68
<u>Heilsplan</u> 66,68
Hellenism 45
   Hellenistic Jewish tradition 58,59,61
Hering, J. 60,70,81
hermeneutics (exegesis) 98,99
Hilgenfeld, H. 13
<u>historia salutis</u> 92,94-96,98
history 71,77,92-94,96,98,100, 104,110,111,116
   apocalyptic view of 24
   as eschatological 99,101
   existential interpretation of 51,77
   as redemptive 27,28,30,40,41, 43,45-47,51,52,67,68,78,87, 89,93-96,98,100,101,114-116
   as two-ages 34,43,109
Hodge, C. 55,68,70,74,77-79,87, 88,90,99,105,115
Holy Spirit 30,46,52,68,75-80, 82,83,85,108,112,113
   apologists 108,112,113
   as Christocentric 46,80
   pentecost 13,16,46
   preaching 79,80
Horsley, R.A. 58,59,67
Hughes, P.E. 84,105
Hurd, J.C. 57

individual 90,95,96,98,102-104, 106
   individual salvation 88,90, 95,97,98
   individualistic 90,94,103, 104
   individualism 88
Irwin, T. 11

Jeremias, J. 27
Jewish Apocalyptic Literature 12-25,32,39,67,114,115
   antithesis to Paul 16,115
   contradictions 18,20,32

messianic kingdom 15,19-22, 114
   synthesis with N.T. literature 13,14,114
   two-age 19,23,39
Jews 67,69,70-72,78
   Jewish 64,69,83,114
   Jewish sects 69
   Jewish Sophia myth 65,71
justification 56,95

Käsemann, E. 13,14,16,22,24,60, 63,114,115
<u>kergma</u> 52,53,75,115
Kierkegaard, S. 51
kingdom of God (heaven) 38,39, 44,56,64,72,78,100,104-106,108
   apocalyptic view of 15,19-23
   consummation of 33,35,49,50, 53,64,74,75,97
kingdom of Satan 100,105,108, 109
Knox, W.L. 57
Koch, K. 32,97
<u>kosmos</u> 34-38,84,100,109,111
   God's reconciling of 37,38
Kroner, R. 3,6,
Kuyper, A. 29
Ladd, G.E. 37,56,71,77,78,83,85
last days cf. eschatology
law 70
Law, R. 34,37
law of contradiction 91
legalism 70
Leivestad, R. 48,49
Little, P. 104
Locke, J. 101,115
logic 32,70,88,91,92,99,102
Logos 69,115
Luke, St. 76

Machen, J.G. 15,20,22
man
   old and new 40
   doctrine of 89
Manson, T.W. 61
Manson, W. 28,115
Marrow, G.R. 10,11
Mars Hill 75
Martyn, J.L. 113
maturity 64-66,116

McDowell, J. 104
Michaelis, W. 42
Miller, G. 83
Moffatt, J. 60,83
Moltmann, J. 97
moralism 95
Morris, L. 14,16-18,22,24,61,83
Mowinckel, S. 21
Munck, J. 27,60,61,83
Murray, J. 93-96,98
  on atonement 95
  on Bibical theology 93-95
  on Systematic theology 93-95
mystery of God 72,76,82,107,108
mysticism 95

natural theology 88
Neo-platonism 1,45,101,115
neutrality 102,106,107,112
Nicolas of Cusa 2

obedience 46,63,75,85
Oesterley, W.O.E. 17
Oostendorp, D.W. 57
ordo salutis 88,90,92,94-96,98
Owen, G.E.L. 3

Paley, W. 99
Pannenberg, W. 97
parousia 35,48,51,53,55,67,107
Patrides, C.A. 2
Paul the Apostle
  anthropology of 28-30,46,106,111
  apocalyptic antithesis 15,16,25,115
  apocalyptic synthesis 13,14,25,114,115
  Christocentric theology of 33,34,46,87
  cosmology of 30,37,45,110,111
  Damascus road 27,41,103
  ecclesiology of 103
  eschatological tension 50,82,100
  eschatology of 14,16,22,41,46,62,64,67,68,72,74,75,77,80,82,87,100,106,114
  key to theology of 27,28,87

  origin of Paul's religion 27,110
  platonic synthesis 2,110,111
  preaching 71,72,74-80
  structures of theology 40-53
  theology of the cross 60,72,76
  two-ages 12,16,25,27-41,43,50,52,55,106,111,113
Pearson, B.A. 67,81,83
Pentecost 40,46
Philo 58,59
philosophers 6,13,70,71,75
philosophy 1,9,12,75,99,100,102
pietism 95
Plato 102,110,111,113,114
  cosmology 3-9,111
  Demiurge 3,7-12,110,111
  dialectic 4,5
  Epinomis 10
  ethics of 11,12
  myth 8,9,110
  Phaedo 2,3
  Republic 2
  theory of ideas 2-9,11,110
  Timaeus 2,3,7-11
  two world orders 1-12,110,111
platonism 101,107,114
Ploger, O. 18
Plummer, A. 83,84
pneuma 45,46,65
Porphyry 70
preaching 70-72,74-80
present evil age: cf. two-age construction
Princeton theologians 88,90

rationality 70,90-92
rationalism 115
rationalistic method 89,94,98,101-103
reason (faculty) 88,91,99,100-102,106,110,112,113
redemption 74,76,78,94,97,100,107,110,111
  accomplishment of 50,95,96
  application of 46,88,95,96
Reformation 29
Reformed 88,89,94,115
resurrection 41-44
revelation 65,71,80,84,87,88,91,

93,99,100,114
   as of God 45,89,91,92,99,100,
   106,107,109,110,113,114
   as mystery of God 72,73
   as redemptive 27,63,84,89,
   92-95
   as special 93
rhetoric 65,66,68,69,71
Richardson, A. 71,75,108
Ridderbos, H. 19,20,27,28,30,33,
38,40-43,45-47,50,62,74,76,82,84,
95
Roberts, J.D. 2
Robertson, A. 83,84
Robinson, J.A.T. 47,97
Robinson, W.C. 105
Roels, E.D. 35,39,40
Rollins, W.G. 22
Rolston, H. 76
Ross, W.D. 3,7,
Roth, W. 13
Rowley, H.H. 19,20
rulers of this age 39,65,66,109
Russell, D.S. 13,16,17,19-22

sanctification 56,63,73
sarx 45,47
Sasse, H. 37
Satan 34,46,49,78,84,100,105-
107,112,114
Sauter, G. 97
saving benefits of redemption
46,52,72,74,77,78,84
Schaeffer, F. 104
Schmithals, W. 13-15,60,62
Schneider, J. 83
scholastic-Aristotelian 88
Schurman, M. 68
Scroggs, R. 67,68,81
Shedd, W.G.T. 2
Shoeps, H.J. 32,57
Shorey, P. 1,7
sign 69-72
Simon, W.G.H. 75,83
Socrates 12 sophia 58,59,61,64-
69,72,75
   as antithesis 67
   Jewish sophia myth 65,71
soteriology 27-29,56,87,89,96
speech:
   as eloquent 58,59,61,69,71

   as persuasive 79
Spirit 82
   eschatological Spirit 47,74,
   108
   Holy Spirit 40,41,46,72,74-
   76,78,83,108
   spirit and flesh 40
   spiritual living 76,106,108
   spiritual men 64,106
   walk in the Spirit 46,47
   way of the Spirit 51,52,100
Sproul, R.C. 104
Stenzel, J. 4
Stevens, G.B. 82
synthesis 1,2,10,12-15,65,93,
101,106,109,111,114-116
systematic theology 87-96,98
   method of 88,89,96,98
   as science 88,115

taseology 50
Taylor, V. 48
theism 10,11,99,106
   demonstration of 99,100
   as theistic revelation 65
theology 87,97,99,100,103
   as eschatology 98,99,104
   encyclopedia of 98,104,116
   prolegomena of 98
   theological loci 87,96
   traditional method of 96,98,
   99
Thiselton, A.C. 62,64
Titus, E.L. 58
Torrance, T.F. 50
transcendental method 96,98
Tubingin School 57
Turretin, F. 88
Turretin, J. 88
two-age construction: 30,32,33,
39,40,43,48,52,53,55,99-101,105-
107,110,113-116
   age to come 23,24,30-32,34,
   35,38-40,42,48-50,52,53,55,67,
   99,100,106,108-111,113,114,
   116
   antithetical character of 12,
   34,43,44,51,52,100,105,108
   as apocalyptic 19,23,114
   conflict of 45,108
   diagrams of 39,53

ethical flavor of 34-37,110-112
overlapping of 40,41,44,45,49,52,53,101
present evil age 23,24,31,32,34-36,47-52,67,73,84,85,99-101,106,108-116
this age (world) 34,35,39,48,65

union with Christ 42,43,46,47,49

VanTil, C. 1,89-96,106
   Biblical theology 92-94
   Creator-creature relationship 90,92
   eschatology 90
   presuppositional method 89,99,101
   systematics 88-94
   theological method 89,91,94
   theory of knowledge 90-92
   view of rationality 90-92,94
Van Unnik, W.C. 62
Vlastos, G. 10
Vos, G. 14-17,23,33-35,37,44,45,50,53,74,79,81,83,87,92,93,95-98,104

Wallis, R.T. 1
Warfield, B.B. 90,102
Wedberg, A. 4
Whichcote, B. 2
White, N.P. 4
Wilckens, U. 60,64-68,71
Wilson, R.M. 61,62
wisdom (cf. also *sophia*) 38,65,69,70
   antithetical 72
   as Christ 72-74
   literature 73
   of God 55,56,58,65,68,71-74,76,79,80,82,84,96,100,105,107,115
   of the world (human) 55,56,64,65,67-69,71-73,75,78-80,82-84,100,105,109,110,113-115
   of this age 65
Woozley, A.D. 4-6
word of the cross 55,56,64,71,75,79,82,107
world:
   and life view 36-38,53,69,107,109
   of the flesh 47,48,85,106
   redeemed from the world 38,101
   unredeemed world 34,42,71,77,78,80,82,107
   worldly 71,79

www.ingramcontent.com/pod-product-compliance
Lightning Source LLC
Chambersburg PA
CBHW072155160426
43197CB00012B/2391